Alan Ecclestone

Priest as Revolutionary

A BIOGRAPHY BY TIM GORRINGE

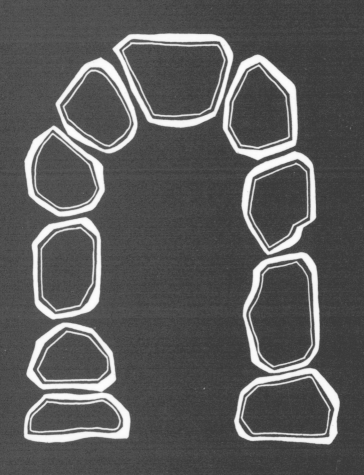

Alan Ecclestone

ALAN ECCLESTONE

ALAN ECCLESTONE
PRIEST AS REVOLUTIONARY

Tim Gorringe

SHEFFIELD
CAIRNS PUBLICATIONS
1994

ISBN 1 870652 21 5 (hardback)
ISBN 1 870652 25 8 (paperback)

First published 1994

Further copies of this book are obtainable from
CAIRNS PUBLICATIONS
47 Firth Park Avenue, Sheffield S5 6HF

Printed by *J. W. Northend Ltd*
Clyde Road, Sheffield S8 OTZ

CONTENTS

To
Phoebe Webb and May Bearcroft
and all the other members of
the Parish Meeting

THE FOOL

SINCE the wise men have not spoken, I speak that am only a
    fool;
A fool that hath loved his folly,
Yea, more than the wise men their books or their counting
    houses or their quiet homes,
Or their fame in men's mouths;
A fool that in all his days hath done never a prudent thing,
Never hath counted the cost nor recked if another reaped
The fruit of his mighty sowing, content to scatter the seed;
A fool that is unrepentant, and that soon at the end of all
Shall laugh in his lonely heart as the ripe ears fall to the reaping
    hooks
And the poor are filled that were empty
Tho' he go hungry.

I have squandered the splendid years that the Lord God gave to
    my youth
In attempting impossible things, deeming them alone worthy the
    toil.
Was it folly or grace? Not men shall judge me, but God.
I have squandered the splendid years:
Lord, if I had the years I would squander them over again,
Aye, fling them from me!
For this I have heard in my heart, that a man shall scatter, not
    hoard,
Shall do the deed of today, nor take thought of tomorrow's teen,
Shall not bargain nor huxter with God; or was it a jest of Christ's
And is this my sin before men, to have taken Him at his word?

The lawyers have sat in council, the men with the keen long
    faces,
said, "This man is a fool," and others have said, "He
    blasphemeth;"
And the wise have pitied the fool that hath striven to give a life
In the world of time and space amongst the bulks of actual
    things,
To a dream that was dreamed in the heart, and that only the
    heart could hold.

O wise men, riddle me this: what if the dream come true?
What if the dream come true? And if millions unborn shall dwell
In the house that I shaped in my heart, the noble house of my
    thought?
Lord, I have staked my soul, I have staked the lives of my kin
On the truth of Thy dreadful word. Do not remember my
    failures,
But remember this my faith.

PADRAIC PEARSE
Easter 1916

PEARSE, Padraic. 'The fool', *Collected works,* New York, AMS Press,
    1978.

The Christian is not a religious person,
but simply a human being, as Jesus was
a human being, profoundly this-worldly,
characterized by discipline, and the constant
knowledge of death and resurrection.

DIETRICH BONHOEFFER

FOREWORD

THERE is, today, a widespread complaint that our society lacks vision. We live, it is said, in a world that is post-Marxist, post-Christian, post-modern in which even what is 'neo' is post-something. In such a disorientated and disorientating babble few thinkers manage both to keep in constant touch with reality and yet offer a constructive outlook towards the future. Alan Ecclestone was such a rare person. His Christianity was experimental and responsive to events. It was open to contributions from literature, politics, science and social theory. The result is a perspective which is both enlightening and hopeful. It is fundamentally practical and centres on the problem of how to maintain life in a recognizably human form.

Biography is a peculiarly appropriate form in which to convey the essence of Alan Ecclestone. Biography is in fashion these days. But it tends to be of the debunking sort – or at least one which contrasts the life and the works. But not so here. Alan Ecclestone's life *was* his message, and that is why Tim Gorringe's sympathetic account is so timely: the life captures the essence and the essence of Alan Ecclestone's life was to realize the true nature of Christian vocation. A vocation is different from a career or a profession. Indeed, it demands a denial of ordinary secular aspiration, a pulling out of the established order of money and status, a sinking in the accepted rankings of social esteem. Naomi, Amos, Mary, Jesus himself – those, and so many others, all experienced disruption and ejection before they could learn to build on surer foundations. Alan Ecclestone had a generously receptive and sparklingly creative mind. He could have made a splendid career in academic life – and was indeed offered eminent positions. But his calling was to the industrial parishes of the North of England where his passion for justice could find its genuine embodiment. Like Simone Weil, of whom he was a great admirer, many said of him that there was no gap between what he thought and what he did. A moment's reflection will show how extremely rare is such a person.

It was from this fusion of principle and action that Alan Ecclestone's marvellous writings welled up. He only took to writing very late in life, in his retirement. The richness of his books is due to their being the distillation of 40 years work in, and meditation on, inner-city problems. A theologian of liberation well before the term became popular, Alan's work expresses a combination of prayer and politics which, international in its interest, remains deeply rooted in English culture and spirituality. The sources on which he drew are accessible to all in his marvellous *Gather the Fragments,* a book of readings which reveals the astonishing breadth of his inspiration.

I had the benefit of Alan Ecclestone's friendship only during the last years of his life. The times spent in his Cumbrian outhouse filled with books from floor to ceiling were ones I will constantly remember and treasure. His enthusiasm, generosity and insight were unfailing. The very thought of him was a comfort and a reassurance. And I am sure that there are few who will read this account of his life without feeling thereby guided and strengthened.

Davidld McLellan
Canterbury, May 1994

INTRODUCTION

AMONGST the most depressing sections of the catalogues of secondhand books are those of clerical biography – lives of the good and worthy who died 'beloved of friends and family'. Like old churchyards, such catalogues are full of names long forgotten. The lives of the saints are different, and if we ask why, it is less because of any especial holiness on their part than because the disturbance they created refuses to die down. The way Miguel de Unamono described his mission is true for all the great saints: it was, he said, in words Alan Ecclestone loved to quote, "to make all men live the life of inquietude and passionate desire, to shatter the faith of men here, there and everywhere...for the sake of faith in faith itself." This is the reason so few of the great saints of Christian tradition would have been comfortable people to live with.

Many people who knew Alan Ecclestone were happy to use the word 'prophet' about him. When I described him as a 'saint' at his funeral a number of close friends took me aside to correct me. Though I understand their protest, I stick by my description. Like every great person, Alan was rich and complex: shy, reserved, private, yet passionately committed, easily moved to anger which could vent itself in withering scorn. A poorly performed Eucharist, or a bad sermon, could cause him to sit rigid in fury for a whole day. Sensitive and profoundly compassionate, he hurt, and knew that he hurt, some of those closest to him. He was a rigorously honest intellectual who defended the Communist Party through some of its most sordid excesses. One of the great spiritual teachers of his day, he loathed theology. Full of fun, bubbling with childlike humour, he was perceived by many as having the steely purpose of a Commissar. "I have no doubt," said one who saw him chair the

Sheffield Peace Conference, "that had it come to the point he would have put us all against the wall and had us shot." Exceptionally humble, the passion of his convictions convinced many that he was arrogant to a degree. He was a man of contradictions – and yet of absolute singleness of purpose.

Alan rarely spoke of 'the Kingdom of God' but it was the goal of everything he did, in public or in private. In thanking those who came to celebrate the sixtieth anniversary of his ordination, in Carlisle Cathedral, his voice broke in tears at one point only – when he mentioned Jesus Christ. Nothing could repel him more than Christian pietism, but Jesus of Nazareth was at the heart of his entire life. Absolutely secular, a despiser of churchiness, he only ever wanted to be a parish priest, and was buried in his priest's robes. After a lifetime of political struggle he wrote four books on prayer and spirituality. One of the finest intellects in the Church of England of his day, he received no formal recognition from the church. Stories of his turning down can-onries and deaneries were untrue. Had he been offered them, he would almost certainly have accepted. Let us be thankful he was not led into temptation.

Alan himself was deeply conscious of his contradictions. The diaries of Julian Green were especially important to him, and he applied to himself Green's words: "No one will ever know until after my death what a struggle I have had to be myself." Alas, he left no diaries, apart from rather random jottings for his last four years, and was always ruthless with his personal papers. But, like Green, he was conscious of himself as a 'Gemini' – two people – having a side of light and a side of darkness, and applied to himself Keats's words about "the fierce dispute between dam-nation and impassioned clay". The anguish of this awareness frequently made itself felt, perhaps increasingly in his closing years.

Alan was a member of the Communist Party for forty years, but he was not the kind of doctrinaire Marxist who had to quote chapter and verse from the Collected Works of Marx and Engels at every turn. Like Marx himself, his nourishment came from quite other sources, above all the canon of English literature, which he knew by heart with quite astonishing thoroughness. Nevertheless, by way of explaining the title of this book, and as an attempt to try and locate his life, we need to turn to those early writings of Marx, the *Theses on Feuerbach* and *The German Ideology*, which Alan himself frequently had recourse to.

Alan believed, with Marx, that our concern is with changing the world rather than interpreting it. The question is, How is this to be done? What does it mean to be revolutionary within a moderately stable, quasi-democratic, society like Britain? In the third of his theses on Feuerbach Marx pointed to the need 'to educate the educator himself'. According to him revolutionary practice involved a coming together of a change of circumstances, such as developments in technology, and corresponding changes in production, on the one hand, and 'human activity or self-changing' on the other. This crucial 'self-changing' was brought about, he said, not first of all by great leaders and thinkers, but as part of the history of 'civil society', the network of families, local groups, regional groups and so on, 'the whole material intercourse of individuals'. This is where we find 'the true source and theatre of all history', rather than in the absurd 'high sounding dramas of princes and states' – and, we may add, of bishops and theologians. History, he insisted, changes here, in the decisions and options of ordinary people. Thomas Jefferson had already seen this in his insistence that the gains of the American revolution could only be consolidated by adopting what he called the 'ward system', essentially a pattern of local democracy.

Where would we look to test such a thesis? Where might the belief in the possibility of historical change which was not effected by the big battalions, but by the weak and the powerless, be validated? Could it be done by looking at the life of a relatively obscure parish priest in twentieth century England – for much of the century the seat of imperial politics? Could it be done by looking at someone who was, moreover, a committed member of one of the century's more spectacular failures, the Communist Party? This possibility is suggested to us not only by Marx but by the Gospel.

Reviewing the history of revolution in the past two hundred years Hannah Arendt demonstrated beyond peradventure that it does not grow from the barrel of a gun. We only have to look at the French and Russian revolutions to see how they 'devour their own children'. (1) Popular notions of revolution, focused on the hero with his bomb or grenade, are, as Lenin said, a form of infantile disorder. The true revolutionary is the one who, like the God of Isaiah, seeks to make all things new, who seeks to give flesh and form to the passion for justice and mercy, and to a different order of relationships between men and women.

The attempt to initiate such a revolution, a revolution which would not devour its own children, is one way of characterizing the work of Jesus of Nazareth. However we understand that work, there is no question that when Jesus preached the Kingdom he had in mind the deepest form of historical change. Was he a deluded apocalyptic visionary, expecting the end of the world, and therefore preaching an unlivable 'interim ethic' as Albert Schweitzer thought? Or did he have in mind a kind of change in human history which, beginning with Israel, would make real what he believed to be God's intentions for human life? If it was the latter, how did he think this was to be accomplished? A popular contemporary answer is, 'through the reconstitution of Israel', as the calling of the Twelve to take the place of the twelve tribes seems to indicate.

Such an answer is hardly self-explanatory. If we take one of Jesus' very earliest interpreters, St Paul, as a guide, what seems to have been in mind was the attempt to effect change not from above down, by 'seizing power' or educating the élite, but by bringing into being new patterns of community amongst absolutely ordinary people, Galilean artisans, women and men, the ignorant and the unlettered, the unknown of the world. "Not many wise, not many powerful, not many of noble birth" was Paul's description of the community he knew. It was through communicating the vision of a new reality to groups like these that the church began, and its effect on the Roman Empire, and on European life in general, was nothing less than revolutionary. When Christianity became 'Christendom' this impetus was to some extent lost, and yet the Church has ever and again become renewed 'from the bottom upwards'. Therefore, although at first blush it seems absurd to speak of historical change effected by the patient and often laborious grind of parish ministry, or equally by the work of tiny local Party branches, perhaps we should pause before we dismiss the claim with scorn.

Adrian Hastings, in his brilliant *History of English Christianity 1920–1985*, is particularly severe on the unrealistic idealism of Christian socialists and finds some of their poses 'frankly silly'. Alan's life work was inspired by one of the more eccentric Christian socialists, Conrad Noel, and might easily incur Hastings' censure. Again, if we want a cause which was lost from the very beginning, need we look further than the Communist Party of Great Britain – a cause to which Alan gave the best years of his life? What historical change flows from an electoral effort which polls a mere three hundred votes? A life which is given over to the work of the Church of England and the Communist Party seems to be doubly condemned to failure. The latter is in complete disarray following the fall of the Stalinist empires, whilst the former dwindles more or less gracefully away, eroded by secularism and even more by economic recession.

If, then, we choose to speak of truly significant historical change effected through such commitments we do so, like Paul, as a matter of faith, and like him must be prepared for the scorn of self-pronounced 'realists'. We know that many of Paul's 'poses' seemed 'frankly silly' to his educated detractors. It is a matter of faith that history cannot truly be told as the story of leaders and led. The captains, merchant bankers, eminent men of letters, the statesmen and rulers, industrial lords and petty contractors – all go into the dark, as Eliot wrote in 1940. History is not so much 'made' by those in the seats of power, though they have their place, as in the day to day decisions of ordinary people, in the struggle for the reality of this marriage or that community.

Furthermore, these decisions and struggles have an international dimension. They were worked out in poor and often squalid corners of the seat of empire, but from start to finish the stage was not parochial but international, and involved a recognition of the importance of every struggle against oppression. This narrative is a story about Sheffield in the same way that the Gospels are a story about Galilee. The setting is parochial, but the significance is universal. It is the story of someone who saw the necessity for revolutionary change and sought to bring it about absolutely in the midst of civil society and through a commitment to the unknown and what today we call 'the voiceless'. He did this in a way with which Marx would have had little sympathy, through an attempt to reconceive the meaning of 'church'.

When what came to be called the 'Parish Meeting' began in Sheffield, on 13th May 1942, it began with the question of what the Church exists to do. A year earlier the Malvern Conference had insisted that "the whole task of the Church is to be the Church" – a strange enough claim in the midst of one of the most desperate wars humanity had known. What was it to be the Church? The answer, worked out over three decades by men and women in Cumbria and Sheffield, was that it was a network of small groups – revolutionary groups – at the heart of civil society. It is this 'discovery', pioneered in the Potteries by Jim Wilson, followed up over a lifetime by Alan, and echoed now by the *communidades di base* of South America, which lies at the heart of this story.

Because the answer to the question of how change is effected in human history included, though it was not coextensive with, the work of the Church, it also brought in the question of God. Is 'God' part of the equation when we look at the question of how human societies change? With the prophets Alan insisted that God was indeed involved, but he resisted with might and main the temptation therefore to take a spiritualized view of the historical process, to believe that through the prayer and the liturgy of the Church alone God might be working out his purpose. It may be true that "through God alone can God be known", but this is in no way inconsistent with the further statement that "through praxis alone", i.e. through the intercourse of actual social relations, can God be known. When we talk of 'God' we speak of an *engaged God*, at work in the world, both hidden and manifest in what men and women get up to.

For this way of talking about God the Church took over a description from the Jewish Scriptures – 'Holy Spirit'. These three themes – change in history, Church, and Holy Spirit – belong together, and form the leitmotif of the story we have to tell. Accordingly there are three equally valid ways of describing it. In the first place it is a biography of a remarkable priest, one among a great many remarkable priests who appear on the fringes of this story. Because it is this it is, secondly, a reflection on, and a celebration of, the significance of the local church, the church in this or that particular place. But this means, finally, that our story also charts the outskirts of the Spirit's ways, is an attempt to understand what God has been doing amongst us in the twentieth century.

In an unfinished fragment of autobiography Alan began by remarking that there had been "no great achievements" in his life, and no extraordinary occasions in it. If we follow Hannah Arendt, however, it may be that we frequently look in the wrong places for what constitute great achievements. What distinguished Alan from so many of his fellow clergy was the way in which he was driven with tremendous intensity by a vision of the reality of the Christian community and sought to make that vision real "amongst the bulks of actual things". (So Padraic Pearse in his poem *The Fool*.)

A lifetime spent lecturing for the Workers Educational Association, and membership of the Communist Party, were not peripheral to this concern for Christian community but part of it. There could be no dichotomy between church and politics, or church and daily life, but rather the profoundest interpenetration, "without confusion and without separation" as the formula of Chalcedon put it. Alan's entire life was an attempt to understand the existence of the church as leaven *within* society as a whole. This tremendous effort led to the formation of a spirituality wholly of this world, and yet wholly related to God, a fusion of *mystique* and *politique* towards which Bonhoeffer seems to have been moving in the last months of his life imprisoned in Tegel. Indeed, if we wish to see where those extraordinarily seminal last thoughts of Bonhoeffer have been tried out and lived, we can do worse than look at what was attempted here, amongst the out of work miners of Frizington and the steelworkers of Sheffield. But this means that, at the same time, such a story is a narrative theology, a lived theology of the Third Article, in which we catch the echo of the Spirit's ways.

The word 'prophet' is rather freely bandied about, but we can use it more confidently of Alan Ecclestone than of most, certainly if we accept his own definition of a prophet as one who "searches for the truth in every human situation and tells us what it looks like no matter how unpopular or demanding it is".

In his parish ministry he anticipated many developments in liturgy and theology which only became general long after his retirement. The parishioners of Darnall were discussing women's ordination in 1948! Though many of the things he struggled for are now taken for granted, both his life and what he wrote leave us with a sharp challenge to the coming Church. He under-stood how deeply alienated the majority of people were from the Church, that, in Péguy's words, "the curés have lost the parishes". It was this situation he sought to address concretely, and not only in theory. Again, long before there was a feminist movement Alan was insisting that the sexual upheaval of the last quarter of the twentieth century demanded a radically re-thought spirituality. He is not a figure of the past but still pointing forward, with passionate criticism and equally passionate hope.

These claims are not minimized by saying that what Alan lived out was the integrity of Anglicanism: a faith rooted in response to the English tradition, which read the canon of English literature, and especially Shakespeare, as seriously as the psalms, but which interrogated that tradition with the questions of the Christian gospel and found the natural focus of human community in the Christian sacraments. His life, and the writings which interpret it, are an attempt to wait upon the God whose history is "now and England", and for that very reason now and Latin America, Asia or Africa. If the Incarnation be true, the universal is known only in and through the particular.

Over the years, but especially after his retirement in 1969, Alan came to be known as one of the great Anglican spiritual teachers of the second half of the twentieth century, a fact recognized by the award of the Collins Religious Book Prize after the publication of *Yes to God* in 1975. At the heart of this spirituality lay a celebration of the mystery of supposedly ordinary things, of ordinary lives and events which to the eye of faith disclosed the divine. Writing of Pamela Keilly, who for many years was responsible for religious drama in Sheffield and neighbouring dioceses, Alan noted that what she did "was to involve both players and audiences in the drama of the redemp-tion of the world, far beyond their consciousness of it, yet touching at times the hidden springs of their being, and bringing, if only for a moment, the whole soul into activity". It is this drama we are asked to regard in Alan's life story, and in which that story invites us to take part.

Alan wrote two fragments of autobiography. The first, which dealt with his family background and schooling, is condensed into the first chapter. A much shorter piece on his time in Carlisle, and the beginning of his practice of visiting, has been incorporated almost entirely in Chapter Four. For the rest, the richest source was the log book of the Parish Meeting, kept both at Frizington and in Darnall, and Alan's own writings. Two of the potentially most interesting records, Alan's personal file in Sheffield Diocese, and the Government file of foreign visitors to the Peace Conference in 1950, were either destroyed or are still kept under lock and key by the Foreign Office, both the victims of the well known British concern for secrecy when this is in the interests of the Establishment.

I am grateful to the large number of people who gave time for interviews and correspondence over the past four years, to Katherine Ross, Rohini Hensman, and Jim Cotter who read the whole thing in draft and made searching and helpful criticisms, and to Professor David McLellan of the University of Kent for his Foreword. Above all to Alan, who is responsible for whatever virtues the book may have. Moltmann wrote that in paying honour to a fellow theologian the focal point must not be the theologian in person but rather the cause to which he devoted all his heart and soul and life. That would be a very odd rubric for a biography, and yet it was Alan's wish that it should be the lines of the work in which he was engaged, the cause for which he has given his life, that should be most clearly visible. I hope that wish has been honoured.

1. ARENDT, H. *On Revolution*. Penguin, 1973

I

FIRING THE CLAY

Seek the beginnings, learn from whence you came
And know the various earth of which you are made.

EDWIN MUIR, *The Journey Back*

As Arnold Bennett's hero, Edwin Clayhanger, stood on the bridge of the canal which linked the Five Towns, he saw to the east "pitheads, chimneys and kilns, tier upon tier, dim in their own mists", whilst to the west were fields which, though grimed with soot, nevertheless possessed authentic hedgerows and winding paths. It was into this world that Alan Ecclestone was born on 3rd June 1904. His father, George Ecclestone, himself the son of the coachman to the Rector of Stoke, was a pottery designer for a number of smaller potteries in Longton. To tell someone to go to Longton, remarked Bennett, was the equivalent of telling them "to go to...". His mother Emily, on the other hand, came from a long line of potters from the principal town in the Potteries, Burslem, Bennett's home town. Her father was a pottery designer for Minton's. They were married in 1900. A daughter, Eileen, was born in 1901, and Alan's birth completed the family.

The Ecclestones lived on Princes Road, Stoke-on-Trent, moving shortly after Alan born, to a six-roomed house built for his father a little further up the hill from the house where he was born. The road followed the ridge which rises above Stoke, linking the old village of Penkhull with the district of Harteshill on the main road to Newcastle-under-Lyme. Building had begun on this land in the 1850s, but Princes Road was at this time still open to the countryside. Beyond what was to become 233 Princes Road cows still grazed and hay was mown in the summer. Both environments noted by Bennett were therefore part of Alan's childhood. There were frequent walks through meadows or fields in which men snared birds in the hedgerows or through nearby Trentham Park, a proud remnant of the high water mark of the Victorian era. Here had stood the 'great house' which had entertained the German princes, the Russian archdukes, the Shah of Persia, and the political leaders of Victorian England. When Alan was born the house had already been pulled down but the park and its tree lined avenues remained, full of inscriptions on iron or copper plates to say that HRH Princess Alexandra or Beatrice had planted this or that tree. Alan's mother was always ready to relate to the children the gossip of such eminent lives. They could choose to go through the woods to Spring Valley brilliant with bluebells, or climb over the ridge to Jacob's Ladder, passing the stretch of water where grebes were to be seen, or tramp along the great beech avenue to Hanchurch Lodge.

Further down the hill, towards Stoke, was a brick field through which the children were always ready to go, crossing bridges over the tracks which carried wagons full of red clay and watching loads of it being hauled to the surface to be cleaned and prepared for making into bricks. The brickworks were a source of infinite delight with their great yawning marl pits, their half-blocked tunnels, and the rows of brick kilns which at night would be blazing with their encircling fires. There the children could stand and listen to the chorus of crickets chirping their appreciation of the splendid warmth, or hang over the railway bridge until a locomotive appeared from the mouth of a nearby tunnel and the signalman came to retrieve the staff held out to him for single line working.

At the beginning of the century Stoke was still the home of innumerable small firms which often produced only a few lines of wares. They occupied ramshackle premises several storeys high and were grouped around the bottle-shaped ovens and kilns which were the best known features of the landscape. Some of them stood by the canals which had been dug for the great firms such as Wedgwood or Spode, to bring in the coal, clay, straw and crates needed for making pots, and to carry out the finished product. A pall of smoke hung permanently over the area and was a feature of the view from Penkhull Ridge. Fires in the packing rooms were not infrequent and the children delighted to watch a building blazing furiously and hear the cascades of crockery falling as the floors burnt away. As the towns grew, building went on apace and there were always mountains of new bricks, stacks of planks and floor boarding, pits of lime, sand, and mortar, and scaffolding around the half built houses to clamber over, as well as troops of children to play with.

Alan's father travelled each day by train from Stoke to his works in Longton. He loathed the dismal workshops, the town which could boast no single beautiful building, and the inferior pottery they were forced to produce by 'market forces'. He had been to art school and won many prizes, but designing borders for cups, plates, jugs and chamber pots was the best he could find by way of employment. A working class Tory, his resentment of the conditions under which he laboured was nevertheless a painful factor in his life. He shared with countless working men a deep sense that no matter how hard and how confidently you worked you would at the end be robbed of something that properly belonged to human life. It made him ill and irritable and lay behind many of the quarrels in the family. His true delight was painting, to which he devoted such free time as he had, and his able water colours retain to this day their warmth and freshness. On Saturday he would come home at midday and go off to the nearby fields to paint, sometimes taking the children with him. In these expeditions the corrosion of his own spirit was lifted, and he taught Alan to look long at the light and shadows on a bleak hill side, or to wonder at the beauty of an orchid or some wild flower to be painted at home, or to name the bird whose call could be heard. These walks were Alan's first, thorough, education in what Simone Weil has taught us to call 'attention'. It was the beginning of a lifetime's attitude.

George Ecclestone attended the meetings of the North Staffordshire Arts Society where he found friends to talk to and activities to join in. These fellow artists called round from time to time, and both their own paintings and contemporary art were discussed, as well as the politics of the day. To the pride of the rest of the family his paintings were shown annually in the local exhibitions. He was not an active Christian but liked to go to church provided nobody talked to him, walking by preference down the hill to Newcastle-under-Lyme. Like many intelligent working men of this period he enjoyed listening to a sermon but he wished to keep the Church at arm's length. The diligent local clergy called, and were not turned away, but neither did they manage to involve the family in church life of any kind.

Alan's mother, Emily, by contrast, had a background in Dissent. The family were earnest Nonconformists, members of the Methodist chapels Bennett both loathed and admired. The harrowing story of Darius Clayhanger illustrates the fact that, though narrow minded, smug, and bigoted, these chapels were not simply the bastions of philistinism Matthew Arnold supposed them to be. Rather they represented an intense struggle for something better in life than the brutishness which the raw conditions of the Industrial Revolution easily bred. These Non-conformists were almost all disciples of Samuel Smiles, a copy of whose *Men who have Risen* was given to Alan as a child by his grandfather. 'Self help' meant a battle for self respect and Smiles's stories represented a chronicle of victories of which they were unashamedly proud. The smugness and stupidity this bred were callouses acquired in a struggle that gave them little opportunity to relax or look further afield.

Self help was only one side of the picture, however, for if Methodism acted as opiate in the course of the Industrial Revolution, as Halévy and E. P. Thompson argued, there was equally a side of the movement which inherited the radicalism of old Dissent. Alan's great grandfather on his mother's side was imprisoned in the Chartist riots in 1842 and knew the Chartist poet Thomas Cooper, a copy of whose poems Alan also inherited. More than fifty years later, when explaining to electors his feeling that furthering socialist aims was a matter of duty, Alan appealed to the example of his Chartist great grandfather.

The radical views of the Chartist years remained in the family and Alan learned from his mother to look at things from the angle of the maimed and the poor. The sense of two nations was always present to her. She had a quiet contempt for the pretensions and insensitivity of the self styled upper classes and a courageous readiness to speak her mind. For her as for her fathers the Church of England was part of the autocracy against which her soul rebelled. Parson magistrates had played too big a part in the wars of rich and poor in the Potteries to be readily forgiven. To be Nonconformist was to claim an independence of spirit which sprang to life in defence of the good old cause. The names of the regicides, Harrison and Bradshaw, were commemorated in the family to which she belonged. She would quote with a faint smile, "If memories o'er their tomb no trophies raise," as if the fact that the memories were preserved was enough. She believed in votes for women and both her children knew that England was the oppressor of Ireland. The young David Lloyd George was the last of her political heroes. In the 1911 election the Tory poster put in the window by George would be removed as soon as he had gone to work and replaced by one for the Liberal candidate!

These continuing discussions over politics or art that went on in the house as friends came round constantly caught the edges of the children's attention and helped to shape their view of the world. They were characteristic both of Alan's own family life years later, and of the Parish Meeting, a crucial part of this story during his long years in Sheffield.

George and Emily met at a botany class excursion, and their shared interest in books, in people and in the arts brought them together. Nevertheless they both approached marriage with hesitation and were always plagued by differences they could never come to terms with. He found her resistant and quietly stubborn whilst she found his imagination freakish and was scornful of what he said and did. She did not see or admit that his imaginative world was part of his resistance to the squalor of working life, a citadel he defended against a sorrier philistinism than Matthew Arnold ever knew. His romanticism was often pitiful and absurd but it sprang from some refusal to be content with insensibility. That their imaginations failed to meet was the source of the irritation which broke out from time to time in violent quarrel.

Art, music and botany made the Ecclestone home a cut above the ordinary. It had pictures and fossils, and a small greenhouse where they grew rare flowers. Alan's mother played the piano, mostly popular sentimental songs, or accompanied his uncle as he played the violin. The kitchen was the bright area of their

lives. In the warmth provided by the kitchen range stories were
read, the adults discussed or argued, and the children drew or
painted on the unlimited supply of backing paper from the
pottery transfers Alan's father had designed. The kitchen table,
whose top was scrubbed each week, was the setting for an
endless variety of occupations. There the children rolled out
bread crumbs, podded peas, carved out blocks of salt, cleaned
the knives, grated nutmegs, and picked out the sugar from
candied peel.

After meals stories were always read. *Alice in Wonderland* was
well known long before Alan started school, but the book which
made the biggest impression was one which had belonged to his
father – *A Christmas Stocking with a Hole in it*. It was set in New
York at a period when the streets and courts there resembled
those of eighteenth century London and described the Christmas
experiences of a small boy called Peter Mitt, an orphan brought
up in the shop of Mortgage and Mitt, dealers in tobacco, and
visited on Christmas Night not only by Santa Claus but by
Kleiner Taum, whose kaleidoscope gave strange visions to small
children. It wove itself by continual re-reading into the way Alan
thought about Christmas and human kindness. The Christ child,
the manger and the oxen were not there. It was this small boy
who dared Two Eyes to come and gobble him up before he went
to sleep who was the most captivating figure in that scene.

The regular expedition to the public library in London Road,
through some of Stoke's most squalid streets, made a great
impression. The building, which drew the attention of Pevsner,
was put up when Alan's father was ten years old. Alan sat at
tables looking at copies of the *Illustrated London News* as his father
chose books, and then, if time allowed, they would climb to the
museum above and pore over cases of coins or birds' eggs or
minerals. Most important was discussion of the books his father
chose. The earliest book he read for himself was H. G. Wells'
The First Men in the Moon, and they discussed that journey at
length. Books which were read to the children included *Hereward
the Wake, The Jungle Book, Coral Island, The Swiss Family
Robinson,* the short stories of Bulwer Lytton, Tolstoy, Brett Hart,
Zola, Balzac and Hawthorne. Comic papers were banned
though the *Boys Own Paper* was allowed. What mattered was the

freedom of reading and of discussion. An omnivorous reader from childhood, George Ecclestone had filled his mind with scraps of history and he shared these with his children. His heroes became Alan's, an oddly assorted group which included Hereward the Wake, Henry of Navarre, Rupert of the Rhine, and Stonewall Jackson! The canvas of this history always remained exceptionally vivid.

The most colourful visitor to the house was his mother's brother, known to friend and stranger alike as 'Uncle Bill'. He had gone to Klondyke in 1896 and staked a claim called Last Chance Creek. He and his friends found gold but spent most of the money they made on drink. A great Shakespearean, he dealt with bar keepers or fellow miners with apt quotations from the volume of Shakespeare which was one of the two books in the hut in the gold fields. When war came he returned to Britain and joined the Seaforth Highlanders. He was shot through the stomach at the battle of Loos and this gave him a prolonged spell at home in Burslem. A red-bearded man with a booming voice, he kept bombs in his room to the extreme admiration of the children, whose favourite he was. He taught Alan to play chess and roared when he made mistakes.

From this home background, which Alan remembered as gay and exciting, he went to school at the age of five in the autumn of 1909. He was taken by an aunt to the infants' school in Penkhull, built in 1844 and standing near the old Workhouse. The school repelled him enough to cause him to play truant the next day, under the amused eye of his mother to whom he gave a circumstantial account of his school day derived from his reading. He was a small skinny child fed on malt, Scott's Emulsion, and Parrish's chemical food, frequently ill and therefore absent from school in winter. The anxiety over his health was real because he had been desperately ill as a small child. Two years were spent in this cramped and ugly school and yet looking back what stood out were almost all memories of imaginative delights. A Miss Podmore described a journey she made by bicycle which set his mind working in ways that John Millais depicted in *The Boyhood of Raleigh*. He was also introduced by her to poetry in the shape of Longfellow's *Hiawatha*. For the rest he remembered only the tolling of the

school bell at the death of Edward VII, and the coronation of
George V with school games and the presentation of a mug.

Like everybody else in the Potteries George Ecclestone got
only a week's unpaid holiday at the 'Wakes', but it was a point of
importance to get away. In the summer of 1911 came the first
remembered holiday when the family went to stay with his
father's relatives in Ettington in Warwickshire. The journey was
hugely impressive. In Birmingham they walked to Snow Hill
Station past the line of double decked trams which appeared like
battleships to the young child. The last lap was completed in a
carrier's cart. To stay in a house enclosed by an orchard and
flanked by a joiner's shop was to enter a new world indeed. They
had tea under the trees and the children stared with fascinated
terror at one of the older aunts who cut wasps in two with a
knife. For their benefit Alan recited whole chapters of *Alice in
Wonderland* word perfect, a feat which perplexed them greatly.
Across the road from the wonderland was a park with peacocks.
Further away was the tower of a ruined church, then used as a
museum, where steps were climbed to handle rapiers, pikes and
cannon balls. His father told him stories of Edgehill, of Rupert's
great charge into the street of Kineton, of hand to hand fighting
with swords and pikes which went on through that long October
day. The sense remained that there were matters at stake about
which you cared and took sides. His mother spoke as Rains-
borough and Saxby once spoke at Putney: "I am resolved to give
my birthright to none."

Usually the family stayed at a farmhouse at Rushton a few
miles to the northeast of the Potteries. In the course of a day or
two the family entered a new world, with fields, hedgerows, stiles
and brooks, and an expedition to climb Cloud End as a great
adventure. To wake up to the sound of the separator in the
dairy, to plunge in the new hay in the barn, and to feed the pigs,
meant one week's entrance to a more beautiful world before
returning to work and the grime of the Potteries.

In the autumn of 1911 Alan began to attend Penkhull Council
School, a mixed school for seven to thirteen year olds, in a good
modern building grouped round a central hall. It drew children
from local streets and from the new garden village. The
difference was already clear between those who attended this

school and those who attended the Cottage School down the road, a much older grimmer building, as if they were doomed to be second class citizens for ever. In winter there were fierce snowball battles with these children, and Alan stood beside one boy whose head was cut open by a snowball with a stone in it, who died shortly after. The background was one of poverty, but the school was neither drab nor uninspired. The Head teacher was a florid Yorkshireman who was the mainspring of that effort to care for children and give them access to things that might amplify their lives.

Three dedicated teachers at this school did much to shape Alan's life in different ways. One stocky little man cycled in each day from a smallholding some miles away. He had a harsh severity and caustic temper, yet when he left the district he wrote a small note of encouragement, and it was clear later that his severity represented a purity of concern for the things that matter, and a willingness to take trouble about them. A second master, bald and fussy, provided magazines of the Arthur Mee kind and encouraged the children to read them by talking about them in the class. A third was an earnest Methodist who helped to develop the children's interest in the Staffordshire countryside and its history, so that being Staffordshire always remained a reality for Alan, and he remained conscious of being at home in that world of brick farm houses, buttercup meadows, parks and moorlands.

In his thirteenth year Alan developed that passion for railways which remained with him for the rest of his life, cycling over to Whitmore village station with a friend to see the engines of the London and North Western Railway. *Prospero*, *Leviathan*, *Belisarius*, *Hydra*, *Clarendon*, *Lapwing* – the last three built in 1846, 1851 and 1853 respectively: these were a few of the engines his notebook records for one summer's day in August 1918. The Irish Mail roared through, the corridor trains to Scotland, troop trains, trains transporting the wounded, or carrying bright red sand from the nearby hills to the foundries at Crewe. Whilst the driver of the 'sand train' slipped into the local pub the fireman, a quiet, friendly man, welcomed the boys on to the footplate to talk railway matters. Alan quickly mastered the history of the line, the names and details of all the engines which had been

used and were now in use, and the internal politics of the
Railway Board. The village policeman one day inspected their
notebooks, handing them back with the remark that he could
not see the point, but Alan found there something "com-
mensurate with my capacity for wonder". The railway was an
expression of design, of deliberate policy, "an artery of human
purposes" which summed up the mixture of superb technical
knowledge, pride in doing a job, ruthless pursuit of profit, and
sense of romance, which marked the Victorian railway enterprise. The polished black locomotives reflecting the sun during
the summer holidays, or emerging swathed in steam from dense
fog, became Alan's Combray, the most vivid site of the person in
the making, an experience rich with the complexities of human
imagination and ingenuity.

Little of this would have remained if life at home had not
supported and extended it. There a lively interest, generous
concern, and understanding built a stable world for the children.
Disputes between the parents were frequent but did not spoil
home life. The decencies were puritanical, a little smug, and its
defensiveness and limited imagination meant that its grasp of
actual social issues narrowed sympathies unfairly, yet it represented an achievement of great worth. Alan was proud in childish
fashion of his father and mother.

In August 1914 the family stayed on a farm outside Leek and
walked for miles on moorland country. There the first intima-
tions of war came as the farm horses were requisitioned and
taken away. Returning home they saw the departure of the local
battery of 4.7 field guns that as children they had seen so often
turning out for drill. On the kitchen wall a large map was pinned
to mark the position of the various armies and discussion raged
on the powers of Russia and France. Each issue of the newspaper sent everyone scanning the map again. Before long there
were Belgian refugees to be housed, and even one strange boy to
be included in class at school. The local battery of guns was
captured at once and as the line of the Western Front was
painted in, it became clear how small were the changes that each
grim battle made.

At Sunday school the children learned about the Melanesian
mission and the teacher supplied Alan with cigarette cards. They

were abruptly removed after the war started when George
Ecclestone discovered that one of the teachers was a conscientious objector. Nevertheless Alan's mother decided, in due
course, that he should be confirmed. He went on going to
church after Confirmation, usually to the eight o'clock service.
He was the only one in the house that did.

Aware of the precariousness of life in the Potteries, where
unemployment was always a real threat, Alan's parents hoped
for better things for him. Alan's father in particular had the
longings for education which Hardy portrayed in *Jude the
Obscure*. Such things hinged first on the examinations which he
had to take at the age of ten to gain entrance to one of the three
high schools in the area. Internalizing the anxiety of his parents
he sat these exams with intense purpose and gained entrance to
all three, thus setting a family debate in motion as to which one
he should go to. The High School in Newcastle-under-Lyme was
the obvious prize, but could the family afford it, and were its
social pretensions too alien? What about clothes, books,
unknown expenses to be set against his father's wages? George
Ecclestone always wondered what he would do if he fell ill or lost
his job. More perplexing still was the question of entry into a
more complex social world. His father's pleasure in Alan's
winning the scholarship, one of only four awarded that year, was
badly strained by fears that it would hardly be sustained. The
crude phrase 'beyond your station' did not come up, but the
thought was there. However, his mother insisted on the High
School and the War settled it. In a world of so many unknowns
it was possible to accept another risk.

The High School, wrote Bennett scornfully, "imitates
Harrow". It had been founded in 1872 on public school lines and
prior to the War took two hundred boys. Along with a small
group of boarders it drew its day boys from the North
Staffordshire middle class – professional groups and wealthier
shopkeepers. Its Officers' Training Corps, its Rugby, its Fives
Court, its Founder's ritual, all derived from traditional sources,
were expressive of a self consciousness which had no misgivings.
Down to the years of the world war it had no questionings about
its status or its future. The sense of strain perceptible from then
on was due to the fact that the rapidly changing years of war

were seen as a challenge to its way of life. Such a school may
easily be ridiculous but it was saved from this by the austerity
with which its goals were pursued and the ruthlessness of its
methods. Its quality was not always appreciated by those who
suffered under it, who resented its petulance and inflexibility of
government.

Two hundred boys were served by seven or eight teachers.
There were qualities of intimacy and personal concern which
might easily have been intolerably stuffy and oppressive had not
the direction been set by a Headmaster, Fred Harrison, whose
intellectual sights were set on scholarship of an intensely
demanding character. Autocratic, hot-tempered, inconsiderate
to staff, childish in his outbursts of rage, he lived with a
smouldering passion for the character of the school. There was a
kind of ferocity in his determination to make it express the values
he believed in. He could shriek with fury at a boy whose
carelessness or stupidity could appear to destroy this citadel of
culture. If he sensed the coming of an age which would
disparage such things, he nevertheless threw himself the more
violently into a personal battle against it. Though afraid of him
Alan knew that he stood for some standards of worth and truth
and behaviour that were beyond reproach. He drove his school
toward educational achievement with fierce determination, and
Alan came in some part to applaud its achievements. He
communicated a sense of dignity, of fine appreciation for word
and thought, of genuine concern for truth. He could read aloud
admirably. Alan later wrote to him about T. E. Hulme, who had
attended the school but had later been sent down from
Cambridge. The letter back was cautiously approving. Only
once in his own career was he made aware of a personal
concern. When the question arose as to whether to go to
Cambridge or some modern university, and when his parents
were again divided in their views, the headmaster blankly
refused to consider anything but Cambridge and stormed at
Alan's mother when she asked his advice.

At this institution he spent six years, walking each day four
journeys of about two miles, mostly through allotments and by
tracks, to get there and back. Progress through the third and
fourth and remove forms was something like forced labour.

There was no respite during terms. Compulsory games and OTC parades were exacted with great care and though Alan loathed both he was not brave enough to challenge them or clever enough to dodge them. Only towards the end of his school career was he rebellious enough to refuse to attend summer camp. When by sheer seniority he was obliged to take charge of a section its manoeuvres were invariably a fiasco. By offering to play a flute he managed to avoid parade for at least two terms, after which he was returned to the ranks. He was conscious for some years of social differences. Pocket money was an obviously divisive thing. Firm efforts to raise money for the Red Cross found him a reluctant giver. Clothes were a constant reminder of limitations. During an OTC inspection the officer remarked: "You must wear better boots than those." These being his only pair they turned up for comment with deadly frequency. The hurt was trivial, but trivialities loom large at this age. As the years went on the social ethos was changed. Whole forms of day scholars were admitted, and it was now Alan's turn to regret the passing of a superior environment.

The war was the background to everything. Each week the Head read out the list of casualties, which grew longer year by year. By 1917 boys who had been known as distant figures in the sixth form were amongst the dead. There was no jingoism in the school but rather an assumption that the war had got to be endured like many other things. It was above all the hospital, at the end of Princes Road, which brought the reality home. It was very soon full of the maimed, gassed and the walking wounded. Also in 1917 the news of the abdication of the Czar was sensed as sufficiently significant to send Alan's mother hurrying to wake him with the news.

The sickly child became a lean youth, with plenty of stamina, who played rugby for the first Fifteen. "A hardworking forward whose excellent training enables him to keep up with the ball throughout the game," said the School Magazine. "Tackles strongly, but hardly low enough. A dangerous man in the loose and a sound 'hooker' in the scrums. His punting might be improved." He acted in the school play (playing Snout in *A Midsummer Night's Dream*), and was a leading light in the Debating Society where he advocated bolshevism as the only solution for democracy, argued for the abolition of hereditary titles and the nationalization of land, and maintained that England was the cause of the chaos in Ireland. During the post war election, when the issues were hotly aired amongst the boys, he first became aware of parties and of the need to take sides. His contributions to the literary and historical societies were thorough and won prizes, and included a history of the potter's craft in the area.

Despite such success his education never afforded him any personal confidence. The underlying approach was one of desperation and he worked hard because he was afraid to fail. The outcome was to become expert at trying to get through various mazes. Some subjects, like trigonometry and mechanics, gave rise to despair. In French, lack of confidence resulted in a complete unwillingness to speak the language in public despite distinctions in examinations. He found later that somehow the whole process had generated a degree of guilt at simply being the person he was. Some of this derived from an adolescent period of self discovery, some from the constant sense of being an interloper in this novel social world, and some from a sensitive reflection of relationships at home or comments from boys who represented a snobbery he detested. It made little difference whether he was successful in either work or games, for he still felt on trial and might still be accused. The sense of being driven remained with him throughout his life, and was partly responsible for the urgency and seriousness which marked everything he did.

He had sufficient mental and physical power to enable him to remain unbeaten. There were some times of exhilaration; there were occasions of escape; there were friendships which were sustaining; but the overall tension remained. School was not so much an aid to education as a tribunal at which one had to produce evidence that would merit acquittal. So with unflagging intensity he collected the necessary material and was grateful or otherwise to various masters who helped in the process. The school library gave him the opportunity to read and the freedom to go his own way and indulge his imagination as he wished. More than anything else he liked to study so that Sixth Form specialization gave increasing satisfaction. Almost throughout his time at school the standard of teaching was poor in the extreme but this was taken for granted. The history master was extremely competent in producing open scholarship results and did his work by dictating notes hour after hour and requiring them to be learned by heart. He also got to know the new English teacher who had come whilst he was in the Remove, H. O. Daniels. Though not a brilliant scholar himself he enthused the boys, and this first contact laid the foundation for what was to be an important friendship. Nevertheless somewhere in the background he cherished a defiant Sinn Fein attitude to school and all it stood for.

It was whilst in the sixth form of the High School that Alan made a discovery which became decisive for his life. He heard about a church in Burslem which was 'red'.

2
BURSLEM
AND THE CATHOLIC CRUSADE

Jesus preached the Kingdom; what came
was the Church.

ALFRED LOISY

THE Church of Holy Trinity, Sneyd, stood next to the Doulton
pottery works in Nile Street, five minutes from Burslem's small
but fine neo-classical Town Hall, and surrounded by pot banks.
In an area noted for its Nonconformity, Sneyd was unusual for
being high church. When Alan first got to know it Jim Wilson,
the Vicar, used the Roman rite and already supported the
Industrial Christian Fellowship. This represented the fusion of
the Christian Social Union and the Navvy's Mission which was
one of the products of the Report on *Christianity and Industrial
Problems*, largely written by R. H. Tawney, and submitted to the
Archbishops in 1918. Studdert Kennedy, 'Woodbine Willie', was
its principal propagandist. This was the 'Red' church Alan heard
of in his sixth form days.

Wilson was the brother of the artist and doctor Edward
Wilson, who accompanied Scott and died with him in the
Antarctic. Like Studdert Kennedy he had been an army chaplain, and his socialist commitment was born from the experiences of the war. After serving in Wolverhampton he asked the
Bishop of Lichfield for what would today be called an 'inner city'
parish and moved to Burslem in 1920. He very quickly emptied
the church of its existing middle class congregation, and began
to build up a working class congregation in its place. In 1932 he
took on a friend and supporter of Conrad Noel's in Thaxted,
Harold Mason, as curate. Mason had helped Noel write the
manifesto of the Catholic Crusade and many of the Thaxted
features were now reproduced in Sneyd. Mason was noted as an

17

extreme ritualist even by Noel's standards (his nickname was 'Proromanus'), and he was also politically more radical. He led Wilson into the Crusade, and eventually took over from him as Vicar. Together Wilson and Mason ensured that for the next two decades Burslem became one of the leading Catholic Crusade churches in Britain, hosting the annual Chapter there in 1932. When the Crusade broke up in 1936 over opposition to Stalin's policies, Wilson and Mason joined Noel in founding *The Order of the Church Militant* which continued the same policies, and vigorously championed Trotsky.

Conrad Noel, the founder of the Catholic Crusade, had been given the living of Thaxted in 1910 by his cousin, the Countess of Warwick, with the explicit purpose of making it a base for the Christian socialist gospel. Dissatisfied with Headlam's Guild of St Matthew, which had lost much of its energy, and with Gore and Scott Holland's Christian Social Union, which was on the whole liberal and reformist, the Liberal victory in the elections of 1906, and the first Labour successes, prompted a small group of priests to form the Church Socialist League. Noel was involved in this from the beginning. The League sought "the political, economic and social emancipation of the whole people, men and women, by the establishment of a democratic commonwealth in which the community shall own the land and capital collectively and use them co-operatively for the good of all." The aphorism which summed up the League's position was that "Christianity is the religion of which socialism is the practice."

The authorities took the activities of the League seriously. When Harold Mason was Secretary in 1921 Special Branch put pressure on his bishop either to stop him publishing its literature or to have him removed. Mason was removed. League members believed in involvement in practical politics. At the 1907 by-election in Colne, for example, so many priests spoke on the platform that one old miners' leader remarked, "It's like being in church!" They were involved in founding the British Socialist Party in 1910 which, in Noel's words, set out to be "revolu-tionary and practical, demanding the whole loaf, and subjecting even the crumbs to careful analysis...before consuming them." When the first annual conference of the party was held in Manchester in 1912 Noel was on the Committee.

Noel began to withdraw from the Church Socialist League in 1916, partly because he felt that it did not subscribe wholeheartedly enough to what he believed to be Catholic truth, and partly because it began to get too church centred. Out of a whole series of seminars on Theology and Socialism held in Thaxted the ineptly named 'Catholic Crusade' began to emerge. Together with Harold Mason he hammered out the Manifesto whose brief was "To break up the Present World and Make a New in the Power of the Outlaw of Galilee."

The Crusade Manifesto set out those things it believed incompatible with the Gospel and those things intrinsic to it. Amongst the former were absolute monarchy, group autocracy, imperialism and capitalism. To be involved in the Crusade meant having a keen interest in and sympathy with what was going on in Russia, though Noel was never interested in Marxism as a doctrine, and quickly distanced himself from Stalinism. It meant being opposed to imperialism – Noel was Chairman of the League against Imperialism, and this implied an interest likewise in events in Ireland, India, and in South and East Africa. It meant being opposed to the wage system, read as a form of slavery; to capitalism as built on an excessive desire for gain; to the kept press and the capitalist parliament. For this group the phrase 'keeping a servant' was equivalent to atheism. They did not want elbow room and comforts within the present structure but to destroy it. In return they wanted England to be a free socialist republic within the community of nations, destroying that 'nest of flunkeys', the Court. For the Crusade Liberty, Equality and Fraternity were not 'extras' which one might or might not do without but essential items of faith. They wanted a revolution "formed out of the matured conviction of the ages" and rooted in common traditions which would "shatter the British Empire and all Empires to bits."

Though Catholic they were acutely aware of the dangers of religion. "The World has destroyed its thousands, but the Religious World its tens of thousands," they announced, and called people away from the smugness of Dissent, the self-satisfaction of the "real Catholics", and the safeties of the Central party, to those who followed "the Rebel, born in the shed of a public house", who "founded a Red Army composed

chiefly of the rank and file, to turn the world upside down and
prepare for the coming in clouds of glory of the International
Commonwealth of God." Crusade members, said the manifesto,
could expect the enmity of the world, and especially of the world
"in its intensest form", the Clergy. Though they believed in "the
grace of the leader" at the same time they considered that "the
Laity are not drones in the Christian hive nor subjects of an
Autocracy, but creative and responsive fellow-workers."

The Catholic Crusade sought to be a working class movement
and its theology was outlined in a whole series of pamphlets,
price one penny, to be distributed to working people, with titles
like *Is Jesus the Revolutionary Leader?* – twenty-five leading questions which pointed you to texts in the Bible which gave you the
answer 'Yes'; *The Christian Religion, Dope or Dynamite?*; and *Has
the Church forgotten? Some events in the life of JESUS the Divine Outlaw of Galilee*. Best of all was the pamphlet *Sins and their Cure*
which was avidly bought by pietists of all kinds who discovered
inside that voting for a party which supported capitalism, or
supporting British Imperialism in India were sins and that cure
included smashing the British Empire to bits.

Priests who joined the Crusade were expected to say Mass
with the intention of the Crusade weekly – "if possible a Red
Mass". All were to engage in propaganda "by means of prayer,
publications, conversation, work in trade unions, clubs, workshops, by discussion in the comradeship of the public house, by
sermons, lectures, individual letters, letters to the press, strikes,
missions, etc. Groups are urged in addition to the above to take
up immediate local work (a) in opposition to some local injustice,
(b) comradeship and help to victims of local injustice." All members were also urged to make "an act of Reparation to Christ for
the insults offered Him in the person of His poor" weekly, where
possible in the presence of the Blessed Sacrament.

The theological principles of these pamphlets have their roots
in the Christian Socialism of the turn of the century, in the
teaching of Gore, Scott Holland, and Figgis, and behind them of
F. D. Maurice. Five central elements emerge in them. First and
foremost was the doctrine of the Trinity. Anglican clergy were
supposed to say the Athanasian Creed on all major feast days,
thirteen times a year. In this creed it is affirmed that God is a

unity of persons in which "none is afore or after other; none greater or less than another; but all three Persons are co-eternal together, and co-equal." And the Catholic Crusade added – in whose image we are made. "Within this Eternal Comradeship all men 'live and move and have their being;' and so Comradeship is man's natural element, and man out of Comradeship is as unnatural as fish out of water." The basic principle of socialism, co-operation rather than competition, was understood as absolutely implicit in the doctrine of God. Alan later used this Catholic Crusade statement for the notice at the entrance to Holy Trinity, Darnall. Since we are made in the image of the God who is perfect community, "The Church should be the home of God's family of men and women in this place, living by His help, in true community with each other and with God; thus giving to the Divine Community the true worship of an earthly Community, made and renewed in the likeness of God."

Secondly, and equally important, was the doctrine of the Incarnation. The Incarnation – God manifested as Man – reveals that everything essentially human is included in the nature of God. We have therefore not to revolutionize human nature but to get people to be true to themselves, "true, that is, to the Eternal Christ, the Human God, who is the underlying reality of human nature." The Catholic Church was formed by Jesus for the purpose of declaring to all people what their true nature is and for helping them to live the true human life.

Noel's critics sometimes suggested that he turned Jesus into nothing more than a revolutionary leader, but this was to misunderstand him. The Crusade was profoundly Christ centred. In the Burslem Parish News Sheet for June 1931 Jim Wilson wrote: "As Christians we are bound to give our first loyalty to Christ, and to be instrumental in his work, and any interest in politics that we have arises directly out of loyalty to him." The Catholic Crusade prayer, which Alan prayed all his life, ran, "Lord Jesus our leader, help us to give ourselves to thee, for the cause of thy glorious Kingdom, for joy or for sorrow, for success or for failure, for life or for death, now and evermore."

The tension between the incarnate Lord and the preacher of the Kingdom was never fully worked out. In both directions Crusade theology differed from the fashionable liberalism of the day, which tended to reduce Christianity to a sentimental Jesus religion of the Fatherhood of God and the brotherhood of men. This difference was underlined by Noel's insistence that the New Testament presupposed the Old at every point, a thesis he argued for in a pamphlet on *The Law and the Prophets* which appealed to all the most respected scholarly authorities of the day. In the Old Testament he found a concern with the concrete political ordering of society which he believed Jesus did not set aside, but took for granted.

Third were the Sacraments. The twin axioms of socialism were taken to be the importance of the body and of fellowship. "Outward, sensuous, material, physical things count," said the manifesto. The use of incense, vestments, lights, music and flowers Noel understood as a sign that God had redeemed the body and its appetites. "If the body is the temple of God's Holy Ghost," he said, addressing the issue of the 1911 Railway Strike, "then those who defraud men's bodies of proper nourishment and proper shelter and proper rest are robbing temples and that is the sin of sacrilege. It is bad to break into a church and steal the crucifix from God's altar. It is worse to underpay God's poor." For Noel creation and incarnation were the two fundamental sacraments, and the church was the sacrament of these.

The man who begins to understand the sacraments of Creation, Incarnation, and the Church can never again reject as 'merely secular' the tangible, audible, visible expression of a people's soul in laws, houses, wharfs, ways, harbours, gesture, dress, drama, songs or languages. He perceives the bond between inward and outward and, rejecting the half truth heresies of spiritualism and materialism, pleads, "What God hath joined together, let no man put asunder." The claims of the senses and the need of political regeneration are involved in the sacramental basis, for to starve men's bodies is to rob the Holy Ghost, whose temples they are.

Baptism is the mark that we reject Social Darwinism, where each is for themselves, and replace it with a truly co-operative society of mutual forgiveness. Confirmation is about the true priesthood of all. The Eucharist speaks of commitment to God's Kingdom ('sacrifice'), the sanctity of material things, and the new community. When the whole human race is living the life symbolised in the Mass, living in comradeship and equality, sharing all the material things of the world and all the joys of life in common, then the whole world will be seen to be the very body and blood of God. Thus the Mass is both the foretaste of the Divine Commonwealth, which is the true natural human life, and a means for bringing it about.

The high value set on the material led to a marked emphasis on joy, and on the proper and natural use of things like folk dance and music. Noel's wife Miriam had revived the Thaxted Morris team as soon as they came to the church, and Morris dancing became a regular part of the activity of Crusade Churches. There was indignant polemic directed at 'church' music:

"Probably most of us were taught by our pietist Sunday school teachers 'not to laugh about religion', not to find fun and humour in the jolliest thing in the world – the Catholic Religion! We need the spirit of those medieval Catholics who talked of God's Merry Heaven and of heaven as 'the general dance'. They knew that human things like laughter and dancing and music are sacraments of God – God expressing his exuberant nature through men. True, our Sunday school teachers did say something about music and singing in heaven. What we could not stand was the sort of thing these pious ones suggested we should have to play and sing. We know that sacred music! It can be heard in Aunt Jemima's drawing room at Tooting to this day."

The emphasis on the material and sacramental also accounted for the significance Noel attached to symbols like flags, which caused him a great deal of trouble. From the time of the Easter rebellion in 1916 Noel made it the practice to hang three flags in his church: the red flag, symbol of internationalism, the flag of Sinn Fein, the flag of a united Ireland no longer oppressed by Britain, and the flag of St George, the flag of a free England, a member of the community of free nations. In due course these flags appeared also in Burslem. For an entire year, in 1921, Noel had a battle with Cambridge undergraduates who cycled over to Thaxted and tore down these flags, replacing them with the Union Jack, which Noel refused to have in the church as it represented a union imposed on Ireland by *force majeure*. Eventually a Consistory court forbade him to use the flags, even though there was nothing in Canon Law to warrant this judgement. Meanwhile in Sneyd the very same flags were displayed, and to the horror of the *Daily Express* the Vestry contained Soviet posters and a portrait of Lenin!

Along with these three fundamentals went teaching about the Church and the Kingdom. The Church, we read in *Sins and their Cure*, is God's instrument to transform the unjust and brutal kingdoms of this world into the Kingdom of God, praying daily, "Thy kingdom come, Thy will be done on earth." It is itself, in spite of the corruptions and disloyalties of its earthly members, the seed of, the attempt at, the beginnings of the Kingdom of God, the Divine Commonwealth. The principles of Justice and Brotherhood to which Christ committed himself and his followers, are not vague 'general principles' which can mean anything or nothing. "The Catholic Church, if true to its purpose and to its leader, must, in the midst of anti-Christian systems of society, be a revolutionary church, the Red army of the Divine Revolutionary of Galilee." To work for that revolution is our job as Christians. To work for it means to fight for it. The fight must be against the devil within and without; against selfishness, greed and apathy in ourselves and others; against the outward expression of those sins in unjust and tyrannical systems, and against those who support such systems. The Church must therefore, the manifesto concluded, be the greatest enemy of the capitalist system throughout the world, and of all empires of the world – including the British Empire. The first and basic manifestation of the Kingdom of God on earth, the first outward expression in social life of the Spirit of God in men, must be economic and political justice. In the capitalist system there is a conflict of interests between the owning master class and the dispossessed wage-slave class "as irreconcilable as the respective interests of wolves and sheep". That conflict is called the Class War. The real Christian must be on the side of the wage-slave class and against the master class so long as that war continues.

The Catholic Crusade Manifesto urged people to help to create a free England in which "by the prayers of St James, the workers shall rejoice that they are exalted, and the plutocrats that they are brought low; in which, in the eager desire of our

Lady the mighty shall be dragged from their seat, the hungry filled, the rich sent empty away." John the Baptist, John the Evangelist, Cyprian, Ambrose, Gregory of Canterbury, and the Catholic leaders of 1381, 1450 and 1549 were all invoked.

All Crusade churches were actively involved in local politics. They were always ready to co-operate with the unemployed or to join with any movement which was making for social justice; trying to forward housing – setting up a housing association, or showing the way it could be done. Every kind of social issue was presented. They sent people to conferences as delegates to maintain the approach from a radical social point of view. The parish paper in Burslem always dealt with contemporary issues like the Means Test, the Working Mens' Charter, strikes, events in India and in Ireland. During Lent 1924 meetings were held in the Town Hall, Burslem, each Sunday night, and more than a thousand people came. During the General Strike Mason was the local Strike Committee Chairman and spoke at meetings in every Town Hall in the Potteries. Meetings were held every day in the church, and it was lined with Trades Union banners. In Lent 1929 the parish took as its study book Ryazanoff's commentary on the *Communist Manifesto*. Throughout the year open air meetings were held outside the Town Hall after Evensong. One of these meetings was Alan's baptism into public speaking. Home from university on vacation Jim Wilson took his arm on the way down to the Hall and said, "Will you take the chair?" Like any Crusade member he had to expound the Crusade view, in relation to the events of the day, and answer hecklers.

All the Catholic Crusade clergy were attacked by the press and local right wingers sooner or later. Things blew up in Sneyd in October 1932 when *The Morning Post* and *The Daily Express* published reproductions of the Soviet posters, along with the text of the Catholic Crusade statement on reservation and the Eucharist, which hung in the church porch:

"In this Church of the Catholic Crusade the Blessed Sacrament is Reserved. God is present under the cover of Bread, but it is Bread consecrated by the body of Christ's people, who know that God is justice and who, therefore, struggle against the Capitalist Imperialist rulers of this evil system for the workers' commonwealth…But we warn you that unless you see Christ in the masses you cannot see Him in the Mass. Unless you see Him in Communism you will not see Him in Communion. Unless you see Him in the workers' struggle for bread you will not see Him at the altar. Unless you are revolutionary against the present evil world, which denies the bread of life to those who produce it, and unless you fight for the common bread for the common people you must not dare to approach this holy sacrament."

"Here in a consecrated shrine of the Church of England," said the *Morning Post*, "a vicar and his flock have for twelve years been aiming at revolution. The creed of the godless is evidenced on every hand conjoined with the creed of Christ. Copies of the daily organ of the Communist party lie on the Vestry Table."

This publicity led to a lot of hate mail. "Dear Hypocrite," ran one anonymous post card, "Either you should be confined in an asylum or hounded out of the Church of England. I feel inclined after reading the Daily Express today to find you and give you the best hammering of your life. In all probability you will get it." At the same time there were a handful of supportive letters, many from Christians fed up with the establishment attitude of the church.

The following April Sneyd, and Jim Wilson's practice, came before the House of Commons, when the *Seditious and Blasphemous Teaching of Children Bill* was put through Parliament. The bill was aimed at suppressing Communist Propaganda and Sir Reginald Craddock, who proposed the second reading, cited the *Morning Post* report and expressed his conviction that children must inevitably be confused by taking together Christianity and Communism. To his credit Colonel Wedgwood, whose pottery was the most important in the area, came to Wilson's defence. The Vicar of Sneyd, he said, was a personal friend.

"He has shocking religious views, though similar to those of the Bishop of London; but often very fine people, whose lives and energy you admire, hold wrong views…he will call himself Father Wilson and wear long skirts, but he is in a very real sense the father of the people of Burslem. I would urge that we should

1. *Wells Theological College, 1930; Alan Ecclestone is on the far right, bottom row*

2. *Alan, Delia and Martin, Barrow,* 1936

not make it in the least degree more difficult for that sort of parson to carry on his work."

The Bill was nevertheless passed by 124 votes to 30. Wilson's bishop, Kempthorne, also attacked him and demanded that he take the offending material out of the church. Under this pressure Wilson finally cracked, and two severe nervous breakdowns were the result, which kept him out of ministry for five years. He never recovered the revolutionary energy of the Burslem years, and yet he later co-authored the *Leap* leaflets with Alan, and set out the principles of what he had tried to achieve in Burslem in 1952 in his book *Redemption and the Common Life*.

Part of the vision he set out there included the practical details of what Bonhoeffer called 'life together'. All Crusade churches believed it important to hold a common breakfast after Parish Communion and in Burslem there were often more than a hundred people present for this event. It was part of the Crusade's understanding that to be church meant to learn what it was to be truly a community, learning what it meant for people to give themselves one to another. This entailed trying to see what this community could do in relation to the environmental structures of the Potteries.

Writing in *The Leap* in July 1944 Nancy Price, a member of the Sneyd congregation and a close friend of both Alan's and H. O. Daniels, gave an account of what it was like to come into the Church at Burslem. The Church stood, she said, blackened with smoke, in the middle of an industrial area which included in its parish slums which should long ago have been demolished.

"The 9 a.m. people's service was an intimate and friendly gathering. It was not only that the Bidding Prayer drew one's attention both to the lives of the members and to the needs of society, but that the whole service made one feel that one had come close to reality – that here was a way of life. What one had sensed vaguely at first was here more definitely revealed: the bread and wine offered up to God and shared by those worshipping there was a symbol of the consecration and equitable sharing of all that is necessary and good in life. No one could feel quite at home in this atmosphere whose conscience was not awakened to the needs of society. And so from the Church to the breakfast table to discuss the problems of the group, the district and the world at large. (I think it was the trial of Saccho and Vanzetti which was arousing indignation at the moment, resulting in an urgent cable to the American Government.) From this to the Tuesday night group meeting where instruction was given, or heated discussions were taking place followed by informal talks and some country dances. The coming together of people of all ages and either sex, gave the feeling of a family...A common purse to which all who could contribute helped those who were unemployed or were more grossly underpaid than the majority. Once a year the group issued out into the streets bearing witness to their faith, exposing by their gay colours the drabness of their surroundings and carrying banners designed to arouse the public conscience inherent in our social structure, and to show from the teaching of the Church the way of Christ."

Alan was caught both by the beauty of the liturgy and the intensity of social conviction. When he got to Cambridge he naturally cycled over directly to Thaxted, which he found almost painfully beautiful. He admired Noel but, like others, found him eccentric. On the occasion of H. O. Daniels' first visit he pointed Noel out in a crowd watching the Morris dancers, and Daniels whispered: "He looks like Pan!" There was indeed something fey about him. Sneyd, Alan felt, always represented something much more workmanlike, much more deeply integrated into the realities of British social and political life. From this church and its clergy stemmed much of Alan's later vision. He was taken into it, and it held him, and both the piety and the theology of the Catholic Crusade remained central for him. The church life of this parish, he was later to say, was the making of him and the reason why he got ordained. Every member of the Catholic Crusade understood that if you were a layman and could get ordained you had to, and although Alan never joined the Crusade he accepted the imperative. From the parish he learned that for the church to be effective it needed to meet in order to talk out, decide, plan, and educate its members on what they stood for.

Reviewing the Christian social endeavour of the 1920s Adrian Hastings remarked that much of it was ineffectual at the time and unmemorable in the retrospect of history. His verdict on the

Industrial Christian Fellowship might be felt to apply *a fortiori* to the Catholic Crusade: that their message was completely woolly – against capitalism, against violence, but with next to no practical positive content other than a religious appeal. Hastings reserves his praise for parish priests like Jellicoe on the one hand, who effected concrete changes at a very local level, and for R. H. Tawney on the other hand, who had a great influence on Labour Party policy, and whom he sees as the Thomas More of the twentieth century.

This verdict is probably too severe if applied to the work either of Sneyd or of Holy Trinity Darnall. No great housing projects were initiated, as by Jellicoe, but there was endless work alongside the unemployed, the homeless and those on strike. Could one say that this made no difference, or even that things would not have been worse without it? The uncompromising anti-imperialism of the Catholic Crusade is also noteworthy at a time when the Church conceived its relation to non-European countries largely in terms of missionary endeavour, often very paternalistically understood.

More broadly, we have to return to the question raised in the Introduction, as to how historical change comes about. We might ask how far the social reformism of the Deuteronomists and of Jeremiah actually affected things in Judah and if, as seems probable, it did not, does this make it unimportant? The fervid socialism of Conrad Noel, Jim Wilson, and other Catholic Crusaders may not have been reflected in the voting patterns of the majority of Christians, but it kept up a pressure on the Church as a whole without which church theology and practice would surely have stagnated far more than it did. And the story of the admittedly sometimes eccentric, but often courageous and costly, stand of these Christian socialists remains as an abiding challenge to our latterday ecclesiastical complacency.

3
FIXING THE PATTERN

> The most essential and fundamental aspect
> of culture is the study of literature, since
> this is an education in how to picture and
> understand the human situation.
>
> IRIS MURDOCH

> Culture, the acquainting ourselves with the
> best that has been known and said in the
> world, and thus with the history of the
> human spirit.
>
> MATTHEW ARNOLD

THE conclusion of peace in November 1918 proved a far cry
from the establishment of Lloyd George's promised 'land fit for
heroes'. After a brief post war boom all the European economies
languished, wages failed to keep up with inflation, and strikes in
many sectors of industry began, including a long and un-
successful strike by the miners in 1921. Unemployment rose in
that year to two and a half million, falling only slightly the
following year, and remaining more than a million for most of
the mid-war period. Hunger marches were batoned by police in
Trafalgar Square, whilst in Ireland the 'Black and Tans'
attempted to crush the Republican insurrection, in the process
burning the city of Cork. Those with money responded to the
deprivation and sheer meaninglessness of the war with frivolity
and self-indulgence. The British Government sent troops to help
overthrow the Bolshevik revolution. In 1922 T. S. Eliot made his
response to all this in the poem which for many summed up the
whole period, *The Waste Land*. It was in this year, at the age of
eighteen, that Alan left the smoke and provincialism of the

Potteries and went up to St Catharine's College, Cambridge, with an Exhibition to read History, raised to a Scholarship the following year.

St Catharine's was at this time both small and poor, and its ethos largely pre-war. College statutes still required the Master to be a Canon of Norwich. In 1922 the former Bishop of Ripon, T. W. Drury, held this post, at the age of 74 presiding over the college with his unmarried daughter, taking a paternal interest in the ordinands in college, and writing elegant but trite pieces for the college magazine on the value of education. There were seven fellows, none of great note, and approximately two hundred undergraduates. All the usual societies flourished – a literary society, a debating society, a play reading circle – and the college prided itself on avoiding the 'pseudo aesthetic' atmosphere then prevalent in the university.

Apart from playing rugby in the first two terms, Alan had very little to do with all this. Samuel Butler eulogised life at Cambridge as the place where his hero, Ernest, was for the first time "consumingly and continuously happy". Alan, however, led what he called 'a very private life', partly as a result of shyness and partly due to his class and regional background. His second year saw the forming of the first Labour Government under Ramsay MacDonald. He went occasionally to the Labour Club but was not impressed with it, and the Union struck him as a show-piece. The college debating society was in any case sure that Bonar Law was the man to govern Britain. For Alan the first two years at Cambridge were in most ways a continuation of school. He worked intensely for examinations, being tutored outside St Catharine's at Selwyn and Trinity Hall, and gaining first class honours in both of the first two parts of the Tripos.

Long cycle rides in every direction in the surrounding countryside were his principal recreation, taken for the most part with a friend from the Potteries up at Corpus, stopping to make brass rubbings in the ancient churches of the fens. During vacations these cycle rides were extended to the West Country, and to Herefordshire, when the friends slept out as they went. It was on one of these rides that they called in at Wells, and looked around the town and over the cathedral, a visit which was later to prove significant.

H. O. Daniels meanwhile introduced Alan to the Lake District. In 1923 he and his friend cycled up to Seatoller, whence they walked over Sty Head and down into Wasdale and over Black Sail. Later they went further afield to Llangollen and the Welsh mountains. The many photographs of these trips show us a good looking young man, usually smiling, bespectacled, fit and tanned. What they cannot show us is someone painfully shy, and scared to death by women. When one of the women undergraduates took an interest in him he turned tail and ran. The energy he could not invest in a social life was poured into his studies.

The study of History which Alan undertook at Cambridge embraced everything from classical history to political science, and profoundly shaped his later thoughts. He once remarked that two thirds of the material he chose for his 'Book of Days', compiled many years later during his retirement, was history. (1) History was always on the agenda of his WEA classes, and more importantly still, he always lived with a very acute sense of historical development, sensing particularly the critical significance of the seventeenth century conflict for England. It was this sense which made him uncomfortable with the romantic medievalism of some forms of Anglo-Catholicism. Whilst Conrad Noel never had any time for 'Dissenters' Alan was always aware of the immense contribution Nonconformity had made to England's spiritual, cultural and political life.

Though Alan enjoyed studying History, it was not until the end of his second year, when his tutor suggested he change to English, that he really experienced the intellectual excitement which a university can provide. It was 1924. James Joyce's *Ulysses* had appeared two years earlier. Virginia Woolf's *Mrs. Dalloway* and Eliot's *The Hollow Men* appeared in the year in which he completed the Tripos. Most important, Mansfield Forbes and I. A. Richards were transforming the study of English at Cambridge, and both were at the height of their creative powers. It was Forbes who had talked Richards out of leaving Cambridge, persuading him to give up the medical course on which he had embarked and to give a course of lectures on Wordsworth. Both men were exploring the possibilities of rigorous criticism. It was in 1924 that Richards was delivering the lectures which culminated in the publication of *Practical Criticism* in 1929. Alan attended as Richards distributed poems blind, without attribution, and asked for comment, demonstrating in the result that most people were unable to get beyond saying that they 'liked' a poem. Richards accordingly tried to make his own analysis of what was· going on when the poetic experience was being yours. Forbes would sometimes wait outside the door until Richards had read a particular poem, and then come in and read it in his own way and with his own emphasis.

Though it was Richards who became well known through his books on criticism, it was Forbes who was the more exhilarating lecturer and whom F. R. Leavis spoke of as virtually the 'onelie begetter' of the Cambridge English School. An expert on castles in Aberdeenshire and the author of the history of his college, Clare, he published virtually nothing in the field of his major passion, Literature. He was well known as an eccentric whom not all could follow, but took offence when an undergraduate magazine, *The Gownsman*, described his lectures as 'ephemeral stimulants'. Difficult to follow they might be, but they were offered with intense seriousness of purpose. His lectures on 'Parents, Children and Pastors in Prose and Poetry', or 'Rhyme, Rhythm and the Reading and Analysis of Poetry' gave him the opportunity to range over a wide field from Pictish inscriptions to castle architecture. Lectures on the Romantic poets went through Cobbett, Horatio Bottomley, the pre-Raphaelite painters and Walt Whitman before returning to Cowper. An impression of what it was like attending a Forbes lecture was written up many years later by Hugh Carey. 'Manny', as he was known, would enter the lecture room a couple of minutes after nine o'clock, his trousers pulled on over pyjamas, his glasses, one lens permanently cracked, held on by pipe cleaners.

"Our course is on the Romantic poets, but at the last lecture he was talking about the Pre-Raphaelites, fascinating stuff, though its relevance was not very clear to us. We transferred to our memories or our notebooks a single sentence: 'One has the vision of a sea of faces of women who have immobilized their necks and demobilized their sex at one fell gulp.' Did he really say that? The student from Newnham sitting next to me has written in her book, 'They had swallowed the apple and it had stuck in their throats.' Perhaps he said both.

"Now he's off – something about the sub-critical pre-misconception that Wordsworth is a toothbrush and Keats is a sponge. Perhaps this is an entirely new idea that struck him while he was shaving – yes he has shaved, and though his tie's not quite straight he's dressed ordinarily enough...Now he's developing the odd but thank-goodness-easy-to-remember metaphor. It is a misconception to think of Wordsworth as abrasive and unbending and Keats as pliant and absorbent – the moralist and the artist: opposite extremes: antithetical tendencies..."

He was, as Alan described him, "about as mad and as sane as Blake", whose "Poetry fettered fetters the human race" he loved to cite. What Alan learned from these two men became vital for all his work in education in later years, reinforcing the discipline of meticulous attention he had been brought up to by his father. For the rest, the elegant discourses of Quiller Couch were more of a cultural event, attended, according to *The Cambridge University Times*, more by middle aged women admirers than by undergraduates, a celebration of *belles lettres* which left Alan absolutely unmoved.

Doing the course in one year meant limiting one's reading. Shakespeare, Dryden, Keats, Morris, and especially Arnold were the subject of study, and these provided the backbone to a lifetime's hard reading. Alan revelled in Arnold's strong sense of the provinciality of English culture and in his devastating attack on the sentimental way in which Wordsworth was read in industrial England. Arnold's ambivalent relation to his own century, so much a part of it, yet shivering with apprehension at it, remained a permanently important source of Alan's later reflection.

From the beginning of his time at St Catharine's he went to the severe eighteenth century college chapel, newly refurbished in 1922, every Evensong. He felt for the first time that he needed the silence and needed to say and hear the Psalms. In the silence he tried to face up to the questions of God, Christ and the Spirit. On Sundays he worshipped at Little St Mary's – at that time the apex of Anglo-Catholic worship – and felt he had never seen anything so perfectly expressed. In time he began to attend the Eucharist daily. He tried to read the great Christian classics such as Thomas à Kempis' *The Imitation of Christ* but got little enough from them. Unlike most other Christian students he took no part in either the Student Christian Movement, which Donald Soper was running in St Catharine's at the time, or in the Christian Union. Soper had come up, also to read History, the previous year, and was a well known college figure, but the two never became close friends. He went to hear Studdert Kennedy when he came, and was moved by his old fashioned evangelism, and likewise Bishop Barnes of Birmingham, and occasionally to University Sermons. More significant was the small group of history students in St Catharine's who read papers to each other. Here Alan met a Roman Catholic student, intending to become a Dominican, who clearly belonged in a different spiritual world from anything he had ever known. His sense of need for this world was awakened, and he determined to pursue it further.

After graduating, Alan stayed on in Cambridge to do the Certificate of Education. He had done a little practical teaching already and was not yet decided on Ordination. The course was run by Charles Fox who, for all his work on educational psychology, provoked rebellion amongst his own staff and students through his icy manner and dictatorial method. Alan himself, however, got on with him. He felt that Fox knew what he was talking about and was therefore worth attending to, though on the practical level the course was very little help. The theory was excellent but translation into what you did in a classroom was another matter.

Every one was required to do one term's practical work. Alan was offered Oundle, but turned that down and went to Leeds Grammar School instead. He arrived in Leeds in January, the day before term, and was informed by the Head that, the History master being away, he was to take his classes, which would leave him with only two or three free periods in a week. It was a near disaster. Some classes became chaotic and the Head, who would come into the classroom when chaos was at its height, was not sympathetic. He was fortunate that his assessor, a Quaker from the Rowntree Foundation in York, turned up for a fifth-form lesson on Mazzini, something about which Alan was enthusiastic and had a lot to say. He was given a good credit and passed. Exhausted, he returned to Cambridge for the summer term.

It was by now the end of April 1926. On the third of May the General Strike began, continuing for nine days until the twelfth. University students were pressed in to service to break the strike. In St Catharine's there were only four who refused, one of whom was Alan. Now removed to Wesley Hall for training in the Methodist ministry, Donald Soper was also one of the people who refused to strike break, setting up a soup kitchen for strikers in Romsey Town, on the outskirts of Cambridge. The college magazine for Summer 1926 has three lengthy reports on undergraduates' strike-breaking activities, written in the style of patriotic 'Boys Own' adventure. Three parties went from Cambridge, one to Tilbury Docks, another to Hull and another to perform police duties in Whitechapel. "The siege of Tilbury had been raised" announced the Tilbury party, rejoicing in the triumph of middle-class intelligence over working-class stupidity. The Hull group reported: "A week of novel, and, in general, delightful experiences, came to an end in fitting fashion, for Hull followed up her very generous hospitality of Sunday, on which day the golf magnates of the district laid themselves and their courses at our disposal, by ensuring that we should enjoy our last night, in which freedom to leave the docks was given to all, in royal style. Theatres, cinemas and dance halls alike offered free entertainment." The Whitechapel group noted that people there exhibited "the usual inane and bovine stolidity of an English crowd." The undergraduates, however, in the face of the Red Peril, ensured the continuance of essential services and the rule of law and order. It was a shameful episode for the University, but arose out of middle-class hysteria, whipped up by the press, which it was costly to resist. Alan was 22, and it was this experience above all which spelled out for him the necessity to take a stand on social and political issues.

Though the General Strike collapsed the miners kept on. Back in the Potteries in late August Alan attended a huge meeting addressed by the miners' leader, Arthur Cook. The men knew they were losing and that they were being starved back to work. Harold Mason had by this time joined Jim Wilson at Sneyd, and it is unsurprising that he was able to swing the church in a much more radical direction. During the strike he chaired meetings in support of the miners throughout the Potteries. "You cannot claim to worship Jesus in the Tabernacle, if you do not pity Jesus in the slum," Frank Weston had told the Anglo-Catholic Congress in 1923. "It is folly – it is madness – to suppose that you can worship Jesus in the Sacraments and Jesus on the throne of glory, when you are sweating him in the souls and bodies of his children." For anyone in the Catholic Crusade, critical enough of the ineffectual nature of most Anglo-Catholic practice, support for the miners was a matter of faith itself.

From these four years in Cambridge Alan went immediately to the King Edward VII Grammar School in Kings Lynn. He had arranged to start in September, but got a telegram whilst on holiday in North Wales asking him to come and join the staff at the end of the summer term as the master in charge had gone sick. This particular master had been shell-shocked in the war and his classes were pandemonium. The education inspectors had been to the school and produced a bad report, singling this master out for especially adverse comment. It turned out, however, that the whole school was in a state which would demand a Dickens to do it justice. The Head Teacher, Webster, was a good scholar – he had produced a number of textbooks on Heat, Light and Sound – but he was a weak headmaster, and the result was chaos. He had a rather sinister way of dealing with things. If a teacher was a chemist he would ask him to teach French. Alan was asked to teach Latin. One or two of the staff rebelled, and staff meetings were ludicrous. Once a teacher proposed after five minutes that the Headmaster should leave the room. Asked to teach swimming the games master replied, "Swimming is not a sport." There were two people on the staff who taught that the earth was flat. Alan was recruited to restore some sanity, and put in charge of English and History, without having any idea of how to draw up a syllabus, a topic which had been omitted in his educational training. When Alan asked the first form what work they had been doing one boy said, "Please sir, I can't read!"

It proved to be a hectic year. Though ill prepared, he produced the school play, *The Tempest*, started a debating society, and edited the school magazine. So far as time allowed he enjoyed the experience of living in Kings Lynn, so different from the potteries. At this time it was still a busy port. Ferries sailed twice a week to Rotterdam, and once a week to Gothenburg, Hull, Hamburg and Antwerp. A large dockyard served a busy merchant fleet, whilst the fishing trawlers came and went daily, and there was one three-masted barque, the *San Antonio*, which berthed there. Three railways connected the town with every part of the country and Alan was able to indulge his enthusiasm for trains. He was free also to cycle round Norfolk visiting the ancient lonely churches. The two maiden ladies with whom he lodged became close friends. They had family Bible readings, to which Alan was introduced, whilst he in turn introduced them to readings of Tennyson and Arnold. Through these people he joined a literary and cultural group and made some friends, reading a paper to them on Chesterton. He also joined the Independent Labour Party, then a radical socialist movement, which met in a room over a newsagent's shop, though Labour membership was very small at this period, and Lynn was represented by an Irish Peer. He kept up the practice of going to daily mass which had by this time become a regular part of living.

In many ways it was a happy year but it was no place to stay. One day the maths teacher took him aside and warned him to get out quickly. The Head was so desperate to keep people he gave his staff terrible references, and after a while one was stuck there. Whilst in the town library he saw an advertisement for a lecturer's job in Durham in the faculty of English, applied, and was accepted. So in the autumn of 1927, still only twenty-three years old, he went for the first time to work in the north of England.

Durham University at this time saw itself as an island in the midst of a rampageous county – there were nineteen Labour seats in Durham, and the annual Miners' Gala, which paraded through the city, felt like a celebration of the fall of the Bastille. Following the strike of 1921, miners' wages were reduced, and as demand for British coal dropped, and new mechanical processes were introduced, so employment fell. The Durham coalfield was one of the worst hit areas, and unemployment was running at forty per cent. Conditions in the mining villages were amongst the worst in Britain, and both overcrowding and sanitation in the tiny nineteenth-century cottages were a serious problem. The Bishop of Durham, Hensley Henson, conducted himself from Auckland Castle like part of the *ancien régime*. His diaries for 1921 and 1926 are full of encounters with striking miners and when he fell ill in the course of the general strike he had nightmares of driving through lines of miners with clenched fists. Arthur Cook described him as "the paid apologist of the Capitalist", which was not far from the mark. This immensely self-satisfied champion of freemasonry confided to his diary in 1926: "The seditious preaching of 'class consciousness' has not failed of its effect. Even the clergy, who might have been regarded as the obvious champions of individual rights and responsibilities, are as servile as the rest. Indeed, in many places, they are mere parasites of the Labour party." Christian socialism he regarded as an adolescent disorder, unable to grasp the essential distinction between the moral and economic spheres.

Alan was based at University College, a tiny place with only twenty-six undergraduates. As at St Catharine's, there was still an institutional connection between Church and University. The professor of English, Henry Ellershaw, was a Canon of the Cathedral. At this time the Faculties of English at Durham and Newcastle were linked and at joint meetings the two professors eyed each other like cats. Ellershaw, whose real passion was music, lectured for only half an hour a week and left the rest of the teaching to his juniors. He never once spoke to Alan in three years. The senior lecturer, Bertram Colgrave, who taught the early period, proved a good friend. A low churchman, the two of them had heated theological arguments, but saw eye to eye on everything else.

Alan taught the whole English Literature syllabus from Chaucer on, lecturing for fifteen hours a week. He particularly enjoyed teaching the course on literary criticism which he introduced and in which he was able to extend for himself what he had learned from Forbes and Richards.

It was again hard labour but nevertheless he started in Durham to do extramural work for the Workers' Educational Association, a commitment he kept until his retirement. As a

choolboy he had attended a WEA lecture given by Henry Clay
n the Potteries and was at once caught by the aims of the
Association. He taught courses on literature, history, politics and
ociology, venturing very occasionally into religious thought. In
Durham he went out to do classes in the mining villages,
especially to Stanley, at that time known as 'Little Moscow', and
o Bishop Auckland, and it was in the villages he made his most
enduring friendships. Every Saturday he would be taken to a
ootball match at Newcastle or Sunderland in order to further
his own education! He was able also in Newcastle to go to the
People's Theatre.

Those who came to the classes were virtually all miners, men
who had been defeated but who for that reason found all the
more need for education. Together they went through not only
English authors and history, but through Dostoevsky. Through
his work he came to be immersed in the life of the North-East
and to love it dearly. The WEA work was a vital means of escape
rom the sepulchral routine of High Table at University College
where the dons had to file in after the Bursar, Major Alexander
McFarlane-Grieve, the prestigious author of *A History of Rowing
in Durham*, and sit in silence under pictures of previous Bishops
of Durham until he had finished his cigar.

As there was no Independent Labour Party branch in
Durham, Alan involved himself with mainstream Labour Party
activity. In the University he re-established the Labour club and
managed to get in touch with some of the students. It was easy to
get Labour MPs to come and talk, and he also got the Christian
Socialist parson Clive Binyon to come. This activity did not go
down well with the authorities. One student borrowed Alan's
volumes of Lenin and, as a consequence of his reading, decided
to leave, despite Alan's attempt to dissuade him. Summoned to
the Principal of St John's Alan saw the volumes of Lenin on the
desk, and realized what was up. "Do you know," the Principal
inquired, "that Mr Gent has left the University?" At the close of
an unpleasant interview Alan was told contemptuously to take
the offending books away.

Alan had little to do with the Cathedral, which he found dull,
preferring to worship at a small wooden mission church in
Millfield in Sunderland, St Mary Magdalen's, run by a

somewhat wild, prophetic figure, Bill Wright. In the University
he was for the first time involved in the Student Christian
Movement and ran their discussion on international affairs.

In the Spring of 1930 the university secretary called Alan in
and told him they were preparing to make him permanent. To
his astonishment Alan told him that he had made up his mind to
become a parish priest, a decision he had finally come to in the
past couple of months. This was not a matter of responding to a
long felt 'vocation'. On the contrary, a great deal in Alan resisted
the move. He loved university teaching and was good at it. His
friend Colgrave was furious with him and did his best to make
him change his mind, but it was the experience of Sneyd which
was decisive. He had understood that what was important was
for people to immerse themselves in a local group, and to seek to
work out what Christian life might be in that group, extending it
where possible, taking the bruising that comes with it, and thus
finding a way to combine politics, culture, and spirituality.
Though it was a wrench he had made up his mind. The next
step was a theological college.

Alan chose Wells as his college chiefly because he did not
want to go to a university town. Chichester seemed to be just
Anglo-Catholic and Wells was the one he knew least about. With
memories of the city from one of his cycle tours he wrote to the
Principal asking if he could join. He left Durham in June and
went to Wells in August for four terms, unsponsored by either
bishop or diocese, paying the fees of £40 per year, and bearing
the cost of board and lodging in the cathedral close himself.

This was the first time he had studied theology, and unfortunately it was within the severe limits of preparation for the
General Ordination Examination. Most of the other thirty-six
students had already read theology. There were lectures on
doctrine, worship and 'parochialia' from Hollis, the Principal, an
austere gaunt creature who left after Alan's first term to become
Bishop of Taunton. The Vice-Principal, Bell, with whom he felt
an affinity, lectured on the New Testament. A mountaineer and
a good scholar, he was a diffident speaker whose lectures were
agony to listen to as he qualified every assertion with the query,
"Is that right?" He was known for the aphorism: "What is clear
is never true, and what is true doesn't matter" – an opinion

3. *Consecration of St John's Church, Barrow,* 1935

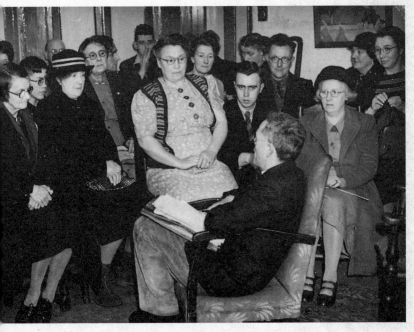

4. *Parish Meeting at Darnall Vicarage,* 1951

associated in one student ballad with his view of the 'Q'
hypothesis. (2) The Chaplain, Hugh Parnell, taught the Old
Testament. Alan was spared Church History in view of his
degree at Cambridge.

Although two such eminent scholars as Evans and Mozley, in
an official visitation in November, were impressed by the "high
intellectual standard" of the college Alan found it amateurish to
the last degree. It was simply assumed that the Church had been
at work for so long that it knew what people's needs were and
could meet them "with God's grace and truth channelled in
traditional forms". The poverty of the theology he learned at
Wells was doubtless partly responsible for a lifelong hostility to
the subject. "What I found most lacking from my introduction to
theology," he wrote later, "was what has been called 'radical
amazement' that prevents 'god-talk' from becoming an
academic exercise. The failure of contact that I sensed between
the Church and the life of society sprang from the end-stopped
lines of her word to the world."

Barth, who had exactly this radical amazement, was as yet
almost unknown to the Anglo-Saxon world (Hoskyn's translation
of *The Epistle to the Romans* appeared in 1933), and when a fellow
curate in Carlisle, H. E. W. Turner, introduced him to Alan it
set no bells ringing. What impressed Alan most on the theological front was George Tyrrell's struggle for truth, and though
he was never himself a 'modernist' he was always both suspicious
of orthodoxy and open to attempts at radical theological
restatement.

He tried to pray but prayer was a curious mishmash of things
that related to Sneyd or to Church of England history. He
slogged away on Luke in Greek, on the Old and New Testa-
ments, Christian Doctrine, and Worship. To the amusement of
his contemporaries he failed this last paper the first time round
and had to sit it again. Very little seemed to have any relevance
to the world of unemployment and massive social injustice in
which people lived. He kept his sanity by walking out each
afternoon to sit on the Mendips, often accompanied by Arthur
Tripas, who had read English at Birmingham, visiting Alfoxden
and Nether Stowey, the haunt of Coleridge and the
Wordsworths.

It was at this stage that his interest in Judaism was awakened. He wondered as he studied what the Jews would think about these questions. He was made Librarian and asked what writings of Jews there were. There were just three books to be had – Montefiore on the Synoptics, Klausner on the Messiah, and Gaster on the Pharisees. He asked Bell what the Jews had to say about Christianity, but of course he did not know. It was many years before he was able to follow up these questions.

Alan was regarded as the college bolshevik. One of only three students from the north of the country, he shocked his contemporaries at a College meeting by remarking: "I think what we need is a little less of Saint Mark and a little more of Marx," and was roundly rebuked by the Chaplain for saying so. He already had a lively interest in what was going on in the Soviet Union and took a number of Soviet publications about what was supposed to be the construction of the new society. This interest was shared by none of his contemporaries, and for the whole of his stay in Wells he always felt an outsider.

The most important aspect of the Wells experience was an encounter with the unemployed, now, under the second Labour administration, peaking at nearly three million. All students were required to be attached to a mission church. As Alan arrived the student responsible for the Workhouse was leaving, and he volunteered to take his place. His predecessor took him down and introduced him to the hospital ward. This was a big room around which sat forty semi-senile old ladies and children. The drill was to go round and talk, and give them a newspaper, or some sweets or tobacco. Shortly after taking on this responsibility Alan went to the Master of the Workhouse and asked if it was possible to go into the casual wards. "Yes," he replied, "but I'll lock you in." When the door was opened the stench almost knocked him down. The Warden asked how long he wanted to stay and he said, "An hour or so." This was Alan's first encounter with the long-term unemployed, and the underworld of British society, those who had lost any hope of ever finding a job, and who spent their lives pounding from one workhouse to another. Here he learned the truth of E. M. Forster's dictum that all men are free apart from those in the abyss. In a way which later caused him deep embarrassment he talked to them about Christianity and the possibility of salvation. He encountered no hostility: these were subdued and beaten people whose world had shrunk to the confines of knowing which workhouses were better than others.

It was this kind of experience which made Alan angry in college. Other students could not understand why his intercessions were so bitter, or why he lost his temper when some of them requested *Horse and Hound* for the Common Room. This sense of divorce from reality was compounded by the Cathedral where Armitage Robinson was Dean, an old-fashioned scholar who looked like the prophet Isaiah and who preached the sermons of Bishop Lightfoot. In Holy Week they used to go to the Deanery and read papers and in 1932 the theme was the Holy Spirit. The only sign of life the Dean evinced in the entire week was when someone mentioned that such and such was what people thought at Cambridge. He uncurled and said: "Well they *are* ignorant at Cambridge, aren't they?" Alan used the opportunity to give a paper on the Spirit in seventeenth century England, part of a lifelong fascination with what he always regarded as the critical period of English history.

In the last term at Wells Alan almost went back on ordination. Much of the year he had felt himself driven almost to despair. He saw an advertisement for an organiser for the WEA in the Forest of Dean, and applied. After interviews the panel told him that they would have given him the job if it were not for an uncertainty he had himself evinced about what he really wanted to do.

Alan discussed his hesitations with the new Principal of Wells, a man called Salmon, with whom he did not get on. The upshot was that, despite feeling quite unprepared for the way of life on which he was to embark, and dubious about the role he was to play, he decided to go ahead with ordination. "The Church was my father and mother," he wrote. "The problems of its condition were not to be solved by disavowing it but by working as best one could in its ranks." On Jim Wilson's advice he applied for a curacy in Carlisle.

1. This is not true of the final version, the material of which is drawn

from a wider range of sources. The 'book of days' was published by Cairns Publications in 1993 under the title, *Gather the Fragments*.

2. 'Q' is a source from which Matthew and Luke supposedly draw.

4
LEARNING THE TRADE

> There is something which excites compassion in
> the very name of 'Curate'!
>
> SYDNEY SMITH

IN the Easter of 1930 Alan had taken a week's cycling holiday in
the Lake District, with H. O. Daniels and Nancy Price, and on
Good Friday came to Christ Church, Carlisle, where Jim Wilson
was conducting the Three Hours service. The next year, when
the Vicar of Christ Church was looking for a curate, Wilson
recommended that Alan go there. Alan accordingly wrote to the
Bishop of Carlisle, and it was arranged – without even the
formality of an interview. The visit on Good Friday constituted
the entire extent of Alan's knowledge of the place – he had no
personal knowledge of the vicar of the parish, nor he of Alan.
Perhaps the best thing to be said of this, he later reflected, was
that he had not chosen it to suit his wishes. Friends in the
Catholic Crusade approved of it, and that was justification
enough.

The *Si quis* was read in Wells Cathedral calling on possible
objectors to ordination to signify their objections to the Bishop in
distant Carlisle. Alan felt he could have peopled Wells Cathedral
with his own misgivings and objections; but presumably none
such were raised, and he appeared for the ordination retreat at
Rose Castle in the soft sunny days of mid-September. Rose
Castle, built of warm red sandstone, with its beautiful gardens,
and set in a broad curve of fields, was reassuring – and Alan
needed reassurance.

The Bishop, Herbert Williams, known affectionately to the
entire diocese as 'Burglar Bill' on account of his pugnacious
appearance, seemed to Alan awe-inspiring, despite his

47

friendliness. He had been Principal of St Edmund Hall and was a philosopher by trade. He got on well with the quirky diocese with its very individual tradition, where father and son often succeeded each other in a benefice.

The Chaplain of the ordination retreat discoursed on ministry to Alan, who was the sole candidate for deacon's orders, and to the one other who was being priested. Alan would not have been more encouraged if there had been twenty of them. The ordination sermon, on 21st September, dwelt on the poverty of the land and the dearth of men for Holy Orders. Alan could have testified to the leanness of his own soul. An incredible ignorance of the Church he was ordained to serve struck him. He could not have felt more strange to it if he had been sent to the Melanesian Mission which he had heard so much of in Sunday School days. A year at Wells had left him woefully ignorant of the workings of the Church and destined to be at all times ill at ease in it. During the service he noted the reasons for wanting to be ordained. The task of ministers was, said the Book of Common Prayer, "to be messengers, watchmen, and stewards of the Lord; to teach and to premonish, to feed and provide for the Lord's family; to seek for Christ's sheep that are dispersed abroad, and for his children who are in the midst of this naughty world, that they may be saved through Christ for ever." At school his Headmaster had noted of one youth who intended to get ordained, "Ah well, at least he'll act the part." At the time Alan had enjoyed the joke, but now he was not sure whether he could even *act* it.

The Church in which Alan was to serve has long since been demolished. It stood in Botchergate in the midst of a warren of dirty streets with innumerable courts off them, a short distance from the pride of nineteenth century Carlisle, the Citadel Station. The church building was typical of the meagre Gothicism of the 1830s, with a shallow sanctuary and galleries. Designed for preaching in the evangelical tradition it was now an Anglo-Catholic centre. Before the 'Statute of Our Lady', as the caretaker called it, candles flickered, and the smell of incense lingered throughout the week. The train of solemn evensongs and masses rolled steadily on. A small band of devoted lay people, a little self-conscious in their Anglo-Catholicism, worked

day and night with the vicar, Bob Bannister, to maintain the
annual round of festivals and fasts. Bannister was the fourth in
the Anglo-Catholic succession at the church; so there was a
certain solidity of purpose, of proven acquaintance with a disciplined mode of life, which gave some qualities which proved to
be important. Christ Church represented a deep Tractarianism,
dignified, not interested in ritual for its own sake, and profoundly
pastoral.

Alan was glad to be absorbed in it and ready to work
assiduously in propagating its version of the Christian Faith,
convinced that Keble's sermon had inaugurated a new epoch in
the life of the Church of England, and that the various waves of
Anglo-Catholicism were rejuvenating floods. If at times he felt
troubled about the relation of his church to the people outside he
remained none the less quite uncritical. Despite his left-wing
contacts in the town, to a large extent he met people on ecclesiastical terms, and it did not occur to him to think seriously
about objections. Nevertheless he got in touch with the Communist Party, one member of which ran a radical book shop
opposite to the Cathedral called *The Wooden Horse*, and started a
branch of the British-Soviet Friendship Society and a left-wing
study group. This was his main source of non-church activity
during his time there.

During his first year Durham University contacted him to see
if he could return to give some lectures as his successor, Jack
Longland, had gone off to Everest. Alan discussed it with
Bannister, but he just shook his head, and Alan himself knew
that the decision was irrevocable.

At this period the need for any form of 'post-ordination
training' had not yet been recognized. There were other curates
in the city but there was no attempt to acquaint them with new
aspects of the work to be done, or to raise questions with them,
or to suggest what books they might be reading. Alan was
fortunate to be working with a saintly man with a shrewd mind.
But he was rather deaf, and overworked, and it scarcely seemed
possible to discuss with him the deeper questions of ministerial
life. Clergy gatherings in the city heard papers read on
theological topics, but these were random samples taken from a
bewildering sea. In retrospect Alan felt that it was the absence of

any sustained inquiry into the purpose of ministry which was the most disastrous feature of those days.

He served his curacy with an intensity which seemed later both ludicrous and pathetic. Old anxieties about jumping through the requisite hoops reasserted themselves to constrain him to be fervently active and to be early for every event. He once arrived at church at 2.30 a.m., having misread the time, and wondered why there were so few people about. Weekday evensongs necessitated singing at least one hymn, which inflicted agonies on him as he tried to sing the first few notes hoping that the congregation would recognize a tune and take it on themselves to sing it. Sometimes his mind wandered. When the Girls' Friendly Society was present he launched out not into their special Collect but into one which belonged to the Mothers' Union and prayed fervently that they might be faithful wives and loving mothers, alerted to his mistake only by the titters from the pews behind. He preached without knowing what preaching might be for, and went on reading such books as came his way. After a year Bannister took him aside and said, "You realize there's only one person here who understands a word you're saying." That person later became his wife.

In Carlisle for the first time he began the process of parish visiting. From his lodgings in Aglionby Street he sallied out every afternoon to knock on doors and engage in conversation with those who opened them, hating the whole business. He felt incredibly awkward as he tried to gain access to them and their homes. With the minority who had some connection with the Church it was not difficult to pick up some conversational links, but with the far greater number who cared nothing for it his trickle of speech was quickly threatened. What did one talk about and why?

The reasons for this daily torture were plain enough. One had to get to know people, to make oneself acquainted with their daily life, to learn something of their troubles, needs and problems. The priest was there to be known by them, to be recognized as someone committed to the task of serving them. All this was excellent in theory, but it was obvious that most people did not require his services in any conceivable form, were not anxious to know him, and unlikely to disclose their needs or troubles to an almost perfect stranger.

In the role of religious salesman he felt still more disadvantaged. He was neither selling pamphlets, collecting money nor appealing for converts. Most people were too polite or too dumb to say, as one woman did, "Why have you come?" They contented themselves with making the going as rough as possible. As most of the visiting was done in the afternoon it was rare to meet the husband or even young adults. It was all too obvious at times that he had interrupted a tête-à-tête of friends, a family quarrel, an afternoon nap or full scale cleaning of the house. His conversational gambits were so limited that he began to hear himself against a background of his own groans at their aridity. The task was to get to know people without staring them out of countenance or cross examining them, and without seeking their custom. The indirect approach commended by Polonius was labyrinthine in character. He plunged into it as each door opened with the slightly sick feeling of one who has no hope of ever reaching the heart of the maze and retreated as best he could when the clues gave out.

Back in his lodgings he endeavoured to recall the salient features of the encounters he had had and to make some notes intended to refresh his memory when the time came to repeat the call. The whole thing was very far from that Victorian practice which could be stated in such terms as 'Read the Bible and Pray'. It was nearer to the ignominious ventures of Samuel Butler's Edwin Pontifex of whom he was reminded when he was told in terms of disgust of a woman who had men in her house and realized that he had thought her to be one of the most pleasant characters he had met.

He fell completely into the clutches of one woman who pleaded for money, who came back to assure him she had lost what he had given her, and came back several times later with ever more and more bizarre stories of her difficult financial situation. 'Give to him that asketh' was a peculiarly difficult phrase, and the streets of Carlisle were thronged with men and women not indisposed to ask. He could not think why he listened with sympathy to the man who wanted the fare to Fort William, but how could he deny him the chance of getting there? Much the same was to be said of the importunity of a gentleman who stopped him in the street to demand £10, assuring him he had lately come out of Preston Jail and showing him with some pride his ticket which described his offence as robbery with violence.

All this was clearly no success story. Alan was nevertheless made aware of some things of which he had minimal knowledge, such as the vast extent of sickness among working class families, and the advent and appearance of death. Visiting house to house down one back street he was ushered into a room where a man lay dying. He was a lodger apparently without friends or family and Alan felt constrained to stay on with him as he rambled vaguely, fading into death. He was the first person he ever saw die, the first to confront him with the incredible loneliness of a person at death, and the first in whose face he saw the softening of features which follows it.

In Carlisle he asked the vicar to let him try and start the kind of meeting they had in Burslem every week. Bannister, an admirer of Jim Wilson's in any case, was ready and sat there with hearing aid tuned in and gave Alan his head. It was not by any means Burslem that he managed to recreate. He realized for the first time the problem of the ingrained passivity of faithful lay people. They came to be instructed, not to participate. Alan got by, though only by dint of having visiting speakers. It was at one of these meetings that he first got Delia Abraham, the diocesan Sunday School Adviser, to come and talk.

Delia Abraham was the tenth daughter of the former Bishop of Derby, Charles Abraham. Both sides of her family were gentry with high connections, supremely confident in their imperial vision of the world. When one of her brothers fell in love with a servant, the girl was sent out of the house the moment it was made known, and they were forced to marry in Kenya. All Delia's sisters but one married clergy, but her choice of Alan was considered little short of shocking. Striking, and somewhat extrovert, she was known for her passionate convictions. One of the first things Alan got to know about her was that she chose to live on the level of income of the unemployed. When Alan arrived she had already galvanized Sunday School teaching in the diocese and was hero worshipped by the younger teachers. She met Alan in the course of her work, as he took a class for the children in Carlisle, and after that they kept in touch.

In 1933, at the beginning of Lent, their relationship gained momentum. Marriage had never been on Alan's horizon. At Cambridge he was far too shy to make women friends and here he was too preoccupied trying to make sense of what he was doing as a parish priest. The growing romance with Delia was not, for him, a question of a headlong falling in love. Rather was he aware that he found in her a reality which he had not encountered in anyone else and which ,had to be faced and followed up, an awareness that if he said 'No' to her his life would inevitably be the poorer.

When Delia went away for the summer they corresponded, and at the end of August Delia got Alan to conduct a summer school for her Sunday School teachers. In October Alan went to preach in Barrow for two Sundays and Delia was there. They went out for a whole afternoon and Alan knew that this was one of the moments when you make a choice about the nature of your life. Things were in suspension for another fortnight but came to a head when Alan was celebrating Mass on St Luke's Day. Facing east, he nevertheless heard Delia's step as she came into the church, and at the end of the service, still with his chasuble on, and holding the chalice and paten in his hands, he said to her, "Do we get married?" They went off for the afternoon to Lazenby Fell and came back and told the vicar. They were married on 17th July 1934 in St Mary's Church, Astbury, in Cheshire, where Delia's parents had retired some months after Alan had moved to Barrow. Jim Wilson conducted the service, to the dismay of the largely clerical congregation preaching at great length the full Catholic Crusade gospel. After the wedding they took the train to St David's and spent their honeymoon camping in torrential rain and gale force winds!

Robert Louis Stevenson's remark that marriage was more a field of battle than a bed of roses has become a cliché. Alan himself described it as sitting on top of a volcano, holding hands with a grip firm enough to prevent the two people being blown apart. There is no doubt that Alan and Delia knew tremendously powerful, potentially destructive, forces in their relationship. Both were in their own ways very intense people, and they were also very different. Delia wore her heart on her sleeve and in public discussions could be abrasive to a degree, though the first afterwards to ask forgiveness. People who knew her in Darnall would say in the same breath that she could be very curt, that she sometimes had a very rough tongue, but that she was goodness itself and 'a lovely person'. Alan Webster remarked that she would say 'Amen' in church as if to say, "If you haven't done it by next week I won't be here." By contrast Alan was somewhat retiring and extremely sensitive, and could withdraw into a silence which hurt Delia. The two of them were sometimes stubborn to a degree which was reckless, though their worst quarrels ended by sharing the Eucharist together over the kitchen table.

"Whatever storms Alan and Delia weathered," said Hugh Bishop, "only drew them ever closer together, deepening immeasurably their love for each other by the generous mutual forgiveness which each time united them on an even deeper level." This was why, to parishioners close to them they represented 'true romance', and what was worked out between them was a love which grew in passion rather than diminished. In the *Communion for married life* which Alan prepared many years later, the thanksgiving prayer spoke of gratitude "for being brought through times of sadness, resentment, hatred, falling apart, fear and despair, for being able to begin our life again, for being forgiven, for being restored, for being recovered, for being re-made one flesh, one couple, when we were being estranged from each other, and from you." For both Alan and Delia, Stanley Spencer's remark about his first wife, Hilda, always remained true: "With all your unlike-me ways, I always felt that you were nevertheless me. Nothing is real me that is not Hilda me." Damaging quarrels, therefore, both felt, were sinning against their very life. "The genuine encounter of persons in loving and being loved," Alan later wrote, "turns on knowing their unique and marvellous if often exasperating selves." What the two of them worked out and achieved was a partnership in such a genuine encounter, tremendous communion and depth going along with a constant battle together.

There is no doubt that marriage was the single most important experience of Alan's life. In his later years he came back again and again to the role of women in society, and to the mystery of sexuality, which he understood as sacramental in the fullest sense. Praying the stuff of every day was the very heart of Alan's spiritual life and eros, the encounter with the feminine in Delia, was the ground of much that was deepest, most true and most original in his teaching. The passages and poems around the date of their engagement in *Gather the Fragments* all reflect this. In his addresses he frequently quoted the passage from Mark Rutherford's novel *Deliverance*:

"The love of woman to man (is) a revelation of the relationship in which God stands to him – of what ought to be, in fact. In the love of a woman to the man who is of no account, God has provided us with a true testimony of what is in His own heart…The love of a woman is, in other words, a living witness, never failing, of an actuality in God which otherwise we should never know."

Through this relationship, in other words, Alan brought revelation and eros together in a way which, if not unique, was highly distinctive, and which became a trade mark of his teaching. "Between husband and wife dwells the Shekinah" was a Jewish saying he loved to quote.

Relations with Delia's family were always somewhat strained. At a time when Christian Socialism was a major force in Anglican circles the Abrahams continued to think socialism an invention of Satan himself. They loved Gore but ignored his political views as a scholarly eccentricity. Temple they had known at Repton, and though they had misgivings about him they let them drop. But the practice of Alan and Delia in sharing table with ordinary working people, or in sending their children to state schools, was beyond their comprehension, and allegiance to the International Labour Party, by this time a truly radical party which believed in class war, shocking.

When Alan and Delia got engaged the Bishop invited them to Rose Castle and said "I'm glad you two have found each other." He then sent Delia off with his wife, turned to Alan and said "I'm going to send you to St John's, Barrow, because you don't know what the Church of England is like."

Barrow was a Victorian new town. It grew from a tiny fishing hamlet of three hundred inhabitants in 1840 to a town of forty thousand in 1870, a creation of the Furness railway, which capitalized on mining and shipbuilding. Although it had thirty per cent unemployment at this time it was still far better off than most surrounding areas, as the Vickers yards continued to offer employment building cruisers, and later submarines, for the Navy. West Cumberland as a whole had been badly hit by the decline in coal exports, and many of the iron ore mines, flourishing fifty years previously, were now closed for good. A partial economic recovery in the rest of the country left those still out of work in an even worse situation. Unemployment benefit had been cut by ten per cent in 1931, and to qualify for it meant submitting to the hated means test. A study of the economic geography of the area in 1932 by the University of Manchester concluded that this was one of the worst hit areas in Britain, and to minister·in any of the Cumberland industrial areas was to face such problems head on.

The man Alan had been sent to work with, Norman Lesser, though not without a social conscience, nevertheless represented a much more mainstream Anglican approach to these realities. Suave and urbane, intelligent but not given to serious reading or discussion, he later became Archbishop in New Zealand. At the time of Alan's arrival in 1934 he was just completing the new church, opened by Sir Charles Craven, head of Vickers, and a good friend of Lesser's. His predecessor had been driven out by a Parochial Church Council which had turned to 'vicar baiting', but Lesser was more than a match for them at this game. He represented the 'Modern Churchman' wing of the Church of England and therefore the style of worship to which Alan had become accustomed was no longer available. (For daily mass he had to walk over to Walney Island.) In the sanctuary at St John's a 'Round Table' was kept and people were recruited into senior and junior branches of the 'Order', dressing up in medieval costume for their meetings. It was in this kind of activity that Lesser was really in his element. Alan sat in church and watched all this with astonishment, and his eyes widened as, in the vestry before a service, Lesser wondered whether or not there was a 'fifth Sunday after Easter'. Vicar and Curate never quarrelled, but they had precious little to do with each other either. Alan got on with visiting, a task which Lesser ignored.

The parish consisted of terraces and tenement buildings built in the 1880's and modelled on the Gorbals, with the docks on one side and Walney Channel on the other. A house was eventually found for Alan and Delia, with difficulty, in amongst these streets, and adjoining the railway, on the embankment of which Alan joined his neighbours in keeping an allotment. Here their first child, Martin, was born in 1935. It was a difficult labour and, in the course of it, Delia wrote to Alan:

"Darling – Beloved Heart – God has been and is so utterly generous to us all this time – that he has made you and brought you here, and then that he should have let me come near and share this joyous, tender, holy life with you felling out all that was poor and selfish in me...the darling baby if he lives – pray that God will put salt in his mouth that he will always thirst for what is alone the real life...These nine months...have been such a true part of Eternity that all the rest of your time will not be long enough truly to repay it to God-in-others."

At the end of her life, crippled with a stroke and in constant pain, the sentiments of this letter surfaced over and over again.

The Ecclestone house was always open. Shortly after Martin was born the newspapers recorded a *cause célèbre* in which a clergyman was tried and sent down for embezzlement. Alan was appalled that the Church should act against one of its members in this way and wrote to his wife, who was left without anywhere to live, and invited her to come and live with them in Barrow. She did this for some months, the first of a long line who, for one reason or another, were to share their house over the years.

Here too, as in Carlisle, Alan found visiting both impossibly difficult and deeply rewarding. Some of the houses adjoined the Vickers yard where submarine engines were tested for seventy-two hours at a stretch, so that all the adjacent buildings shook! It was not surprising that some of the inhabitants suffered from 'bad nerves'. Like every curate at this period Alan was also asked to start a youth club, another practicality which Wells had not touched on. The announcement was given out in the local schools and youngsters poured in, as there was no alternative provision for them in the town. In this line Alan learned a great deal very quickly, buying a whistle after the very first meeting!

The question of peace was, along with unemployment, first on the political agenda. Hitler had come to power in January 1933 and withdrawn from the League of Nations in October. As Germany began to rearm, talk of a possible war was inevitable and this produced horrified reactions. In February 1933 the Oxford Union voted that "This house will in no circumstances fight for King and Country". From St Martin-in-the-Fields Dick Sheppard founded the Peace Pledge Union in October 1934 which collected 80 000 pledges never to fight in another war. In the same year the League of Nations Union organized a peace ballot which Alan promoted in Barrow Island. It meant going to every house twice to fill in a ballot form with questions about peace and rearmament.

People in Barrow were highly ambivalent about all this. War meant employment, as the shipyards would be full. The head of Vickers, Sir Charles Craven, assembled his work force as the November election approached in 1935, and told them that unless there was a Conservative government they would not get work. Considering on the one hand Baldwin's notorious pusillanimity on the question of rearmament, and Ernest Bevin's victory over Lansbury and the peace party at the Labour conference in that year, this was rather less than honest. Nevertheless the sitting MP for Barrow, Sir Jonah Walker Smith, who had won the seat for the Tories in 1931, was an advocate of rearmament. Vickers was promised the contract for building submarines, which was a great catch, and meant work for years. As the election approached Alan publicly challenged Walker Smith to say where he stood on the peace issue, and this was gleefully taken up by the *North Western Daily Mail*, which headed its inside page: "Sir Jonah Walker Smith and the Curate".

In the public meeting where he addressed Alan's questions he appeared unruffled, but when he came to call on Alan a little later it was a different story. Though he began by saying that it did not matter what Alan did, he was actually not so sure. Whilst the local people might elect a Tory Member of Parliament because they were persuaded that this was necessary to keep their jobs, they elected a Labour council, and the Mayor of Barrow was a pacifist. He wanted to know therefore why Alan had intervened in politics. When Alan in turn tried to pin him down on what he thought was good for the people of Barrow Island he replied "That doesn't concern you in the slightest – you stick to religion" – and the visit ended in a shouting match. Nevertheless, come November, Walker Smith was duly re-elected.

Early the next year the Bishop of Carlisle summoned Alan to Rose Castle. When he arrived the Bishop said, "I have the patrons of St John's, Keswick, in the next room. Are you interested?" To the Bishop's intense chagrin Alan replied "No." Their next meeting was in Barrow in the summer. The Bishop greeted him by saying, "You're a contumacious creature, aren't you!" Alan said, "Am I?" to which he replied "Yes, I think you are. Will you go to Frizington if I offer it to you?" Alan knew Frizington as an area of mass unemployment and real deprivation and therefore said 'Yes' right away. The family moved two months later.

5
DISCOVERING COMMUNITY

> In what way are we the *ekklesia*, those who
> are called forth, not regarding ourselves
> from a religious point of view as specially
> favoured, but rather as belonging wholly
> to the world?
>
> DIETRICH BONHOEFFER

IN September 1936, a month after the birth of their second son, Giles, the Ecclestones moved to Frizington. It was to be the most beautiful vicarage they ever had – a large Edwardian house in mock Tudor style, with a fine garden which both enjoyed tending, overlooking a farm on the opposite side of the road. Here, in April 1939, their third son, Jacob, was born. In August of that year a Jewish refugee, Herbert Neuwalder, joined them and became part of the family until 1947. They brought with them too, from Barrow, the daughter of one of their neighbours, Dorothy Steele. For some years she lived with them, again as part of the family, and delighted them with her fresh appreciation of what was for her a 'brave new world'. With his own memories of being force fed at school, and with the garden to take advantage of, Alan decided to keep the children from school until they were six, teaching them to read himself. They camped in the garden a good deal, making camp fires amongst the trees, and when Herbert was suspected of having diphtheria he was 'quarantined' in a tent with Dorothy for six weeks together!

From the start the vicarage became the 'parish house', and meetings were held in the sitting room. The former 'tradesmen's entrance' was done away with and everyone was brought in by the front door. Whoever stayed there was included in the family prayers in the morning and in the wholesome, plain meals Delia

prided herself on cooking. There was a Franciscan aspect to
Delia which stayed with her all her life: she would take the
clothes off her back to give to someone who needed them, and
once took a woman who had been battered to bed with her, to
comfort her. From their own salary, which was not lavish, they
managed to pay for unemployed people to take holidays.

Frizington lay some five miles east of Whitehaven, and a
couple of miles north of Cleator Moor. Like Barrow it was the
product of Victorian expansion, growing from a hamlet of under
three hundred people in 1831 to six and a half thousand by 1881.
The area was rich in iron, and there were twenty-three iron ore
pits in the parish which had, at their peak, produced more than
150000 tons of ore a year. By 1936 all of these were closed, and
unemployment was almost total. There were at this period, said
Cole and Postgate, in *The Common People*, 'areas of extreme
wretchedness' in which the effects of idleness, poverty and the
dole made the human decay of an area worse than the material
decay. Frizington was one such place. To the extent that it was
possible to mobilize protest about unemployment, Alan joined
in. When there was a march of the unemployed through West
Cumberland he took part and was put up to speak in Whitehaven. This raised the usual flurry of indignation on the part of
those who could not see that such activity could have anything to
do with being a pastor. Tuberculosis was rife in the village, and
Alan had to bury whole families. When they took in two girls
whose parents had died, their own son Giles contracted the
disease. Both girls died, as the illness was already far advanced,
but after an operation, and a spell of convalescence in Norway,
Giles survived.

St Paul's, Frizington, had been built in the 1860s to meet the
needs of the rising population. It was built in the Early English
style, using the local red sandstone. Electricity was only installed
in Alan's second year. The village knew fierce antagonism
between Protestant and Catholic, as workers for the mines had
been brought over from Northern Ireland in the previous
century. As Alan read the Thirty-Nine Articles in the course of
his induction, he heard a great grunt of approval as he came to
the reference in the Prayer Book to the 'Bishop of Rome'. Alan
encountered hostility from the Protestant Orange Lodge on one

side, and from Catholic clergy on the other, who refused to
acknowledge his presence. His introduction of altar hangings led
some of those with Protestant sympathies to leave the church,
whilst on the Catholic side there were many problems arising
from so-called 'mixed marriages'. In a situation where Cardinal
Hinsley of Westminster was reproved for praying the Lord's
Prayer together with Anglicans, it is hardly surprising that in an
area as remote as this a Protestant woman might not be allowed
into the room whilst her Catholic husband received the last rites.
The people themselves did not necessarily respect these divi-
sions. Warned by a Protestant in the course of visiting that the
next door house was Catholic Alan quietly passed by, only to be
indignantly hailed back and installed in a chair for tea!

The regular round of visiting, which Alan started at once, was
the background of all else. It was possible to visit every house in
the parish, mostly ranged in long rows of miners' cottages, once
a quarter. The purpose of such visits, he was clear, was not
recruitment, but simply to get to know whoever lived in the
parish as people, to find out where they were, and what their
background was. It meant that he was able to get to know the
housebound, and families with serious problems such as child
battering, with an intimacy possible in no other way. At the
same time it was the essential starting point for all social and
educational work.

Some of this was simple charity work, and here Alan ran into
some trouble. A local Tory lady, Claribel Curwen, had for some
time been bringing second-hand clothing for distribution. This
had been done through the Labour party bosses, but was now
transferred to the vicarage, as she realized that a wider range of
people would have easier access. Parcels were made up and the
clothes taken out at night so that people should not know how
the distribution was going. This upset the Labour bosses who
made relationships difficult in all sorts of other areas. Claribel
Curwen meanwhile became a great friend, coming to the
vicarage to borrow books – the only person who ever asked to
borrow the novels of Samuel Richardson!

The Society of Friends were already active in the area and
supplied a hut which could be used for classes in dressmaking,
cobbling or other alternative forms of employment. They drew

into West Cumbria a group of intellectuals who were keen to
help. The Balliol anthropologist Thomas Hodgkin had a house
in Whitehaven and was involved in a settlement in Maryport
He got people like the Master of Balliol, A. D. Lindsay, to come
and talk about Plato, and Eric Gill to talk on the philosophy of
work, addressing large numbers of working people. Alan himself
offered courses on 'The history of our own times', and some of
the men commented, "Everything you said was true." Hodgkin
stayed several times at the vicarage and supplied vivid information about the various world situations in which he was active
especially Spain. The Spanish Civil War began in 1936 and Alan
became Chairman of the Food Ship for Spain Committee. That
year fifty children from the Basque region were brought to the
area. The previous year Victor Gollancz had started the Left
Book Club, and Alan started a branch of this as soon as he
arrived in Frizington, at the meetings of which the Book of the
Month was taken and discussed. Gollancz himself came and
spoke to a packed crowd in the local cinema in 1938, immediately after Munich, making clear that appeasement was not a
possibility. Alan's support for the Peace Pledge Union now had
to bow before the turn of events in Germany. In the agonized
debates of the Christian Left over the peace issue at this time he
did not feel able to follow the consistent pacifism of Charles
Raven or Donald Soper.

In Frizington Alan resumed the work for the WEA which he
had been forced to abandon during his four years as a curate
Cumberland was under the same extramural board as Durham
so he was already well known. From this time he continued
WEA work right up to his retirement and no class of his ever
failed for lack of numbers. He offered classes on political history
from Versailles to the present, and on sociology, travelling by
bus to Egremont or Whitehaven, accompanied usually by Delia
Unemployment meant that people had time on their hands, and
where there was still the motivation for learning the classes were
keen and hard-working.

War was on the horizon from the moment they arrived in the
new parish. In that year Italy invaded Abyssinia. In the following
year Japan invaded Manchuria. In 1938 Hitler annexed Austria
and moved into Czechoslovakia. In this situation of crisis Barth

said in Germany: "The most important thing is to keep doing theology." In something of the same spirit Alan began to take further his exploration of what being church might mean. His background was in the liturgical and political vitality of Sneyd, which already had a regular church meeting in the vicarage. Gabriel Hebert published *The Parish Communion* in 1937, drawing on a number of existing experiments and advocating that in all parishes a 9 a.m. Eucharist ought to be the main service. Jim Wilson reviewed it in *The Church Militant,* praising it for its stand against individualism and clericalism but critical of its lack of social or political vision.

Taking stock after the first few months Alan felt that the church had little sense of being a community. The elderly, especially, had simply been left to their own devices. He sought, therefore, both to nurture a community sense and to introduce those liturgical changes Hebert was advocating. He made a beginning with the women's meeting, which met monthly during the winter of 1936, and was then reconstituted on a weekly basis in the new year, to meet for general discussion without speakers. That spring Alan got H. O. Daniels up to lead a Parish Convention, to which about forty people came, and Jim Wilson followed in 1938.

Alan's experience at Sneyd, and the ideals of the Catholic Crusade, were clearly decisive factors in what he set out to do. Attendance at the conventions grew to eighty or ninety people, and the group took a major part in raising money for the food ship to Spain and for Czechoslovak relief. The subjects for discussion ranged from problems affecting West Cumberland, to the issues of Ireland, which formally became an independent republic at the end of 1937, to Palestine, Germany and India, and to the questions of prayer and church services. The group was not for the ideologically like-minded, and discussion was often difficult. George Bell's pamphlet on 'A Christian International Order', for example, produced only sticky silence, partly because its mode of argument was above people's heads. Alan noted in the log book in June 1941: "We have not yet got past the 'We must win the war first' attitude. We have not yet convinced people that even winning the war demands a wholly new attitude to life." Similarly on India: "India is also remote."

Meetings naturally tended to come to life when they addressed local problems. Nevertheless the issues of the international community were kept on the agenda the whole time. From the start the group was in principle ecumenical. A number of Roman Catholics attended in Frizington, and Methodists and Congregationalists in other centres.

From these meetings grew the practice of a monthly Parish Communion. Matins was not discontinued for two years, but at the end of that time the 9.30 a.m. Parish Communion became the principal service. Delia made banners to hang from the gallery, vestments for the Eucharist, and frontals for the altar, all of which seemed dangerously 'popish' to the intensely Protestant susceptibilities of the area. "Well, you've ruined our church now!" was how the Treasurer greeted the first frontal. The first time servers were used one family walked out and never came back. When a Faculty was obtained for two candlesticks in 1940 more people left. Though the introduction of the liturgical calendar met with little enthusiasm the weekly Eucharist for the Confessing Church in Germany met with a more interested response. From 1939 onwards a photo of Niemöller was kept in the church, and this was a gesture people appreciated.

A third parish convention was due to be held in September 1939 but the outbreak of war caused its abandonment. Blackout restrictions meant that large meetings had to be abandoned. A smaller group therefore met for a twelve-week course on the historical study of the New Testament under the auspices of the WEA. When this came to an end the members migrated to the vicarage and continued as a discussion group.

A new and more spirited phase of group activity began with the Parish Convention held at the beginning of September 1940, led again by Jim Wilson. To the Convention came representatives from ten other parishes, including Egremont, Moresby, Workington, Millom, Ulverston and Whitehaven. H. O. Daniels also joined them for a time. Discussion during this convention was lively and a much larger number of people attended it.

From now onwards the parish group met without a break, and in all weathers, from a wild snowy night in January, when only twelve turned up, to beautiful sunny evenings in the Lake District valleys in September. During the autumn months great keenness was shown in the meetings, and visitors from Egremont, Kells and Moresby were frequently welcomed.

Six neighbouring parishes joined in the experiment and they produced a leaflet in common called *The Leap*, printed by a firm in Burnley. 'By the help of my God I leap over the wall,' was the motif on the leaflets, drawing attention to the fact that to be truly the Church they must be non-parochial, in the pejorative sense, and 'leap over the wall' both between parish and parish and between so-called sacred and secular concerns. The incumbents of the six parishes did not all see things in one way, but they at least faced in a similar direction. In all of these parishes similar groups were beginning. The first number of *The Leap* appeared in December 1940 at the height of the 'phoney war'.

The group also began to prepare for public meetings – notably for a missionary lecture at Egremont at which the head of the Cawnpore Mission spoke. A number of the group went armed with questions, and a knowledge of Edmund Thompson's books on India, and found the value of it greatly increased. They did the same at a Ministry of Information meeting addressed by Leonard Behrens at which members from Frizington formed half the audience. A local Ministry of Information committee was formed and two members from Frizington were appointed. Complaints were then more easily forwarded from the group to the Committee.

The need to build networks between different parishes was extended even further when links were made with St John's, Newcastle. A number of children from South Shields had been evacuated to the parish in 1939, and more in 1940. Extending the '*Leap*' project in their direction was a natural step. Groups of parishioners made return visits across the country, often for the first time. The rapscallion children, and the freedom of the women to go for a drink in a pub whenever they felt inclined, all shocked the Cumberland people deeply. Similar parish exchanges were also made from Carlisle and Barnsley. "We cannot but feel that it forms a landmark in the development of our group activity," Alan noted in his log book.

From the moment war broke out the issue of the kind of society people would want to see when it was over was high on the agenda. The Malvern Conference, summoned by William

Temple in January 1941, addressed this question in the light of the acute social problems of the previous decade. Alan attended as one of three representatives from Carlisle diocese. As a conference the meeting was a failure, lasting less than three days and being grossly overloaded with substantial papers. When Temple summed up 'the mind of the meeting' to the bewildered delegates, Alec Vidler stood up and said, "I dissent from every word of it!" and in this he spoke for many. Though Alan agreed with much that was said, especially Richard Acland's plea for common ownership, he felt that what was missing "was a deep sense of God at work in the world." Like Vidler he was critical of Temple's leadership. Alan considered that when Temple died in 1944 he had not prepared church people to develop a new sense of fellowship, nor realized that the Church had to reckon effectively with a post-Christian society.

Nevertheless, in the course of the conference Temple had sidled up to him and said, "Tell me what you've been talking about at your Parish Meeting." His informant may have been Gabriel Hebert, the leading liturgist of the day, who became a frequent visitor to Frizington and who sought "to sow the seeds of this conflagration everywhere." To some extent what was happening here simply reflected the national mood. Adrian Hastings noted that the intense sense of unity engendered by the struggle against Germany enabled people to transcend the inherited follies of the past, so that 1940 and 1941 "provided a rare moment of *communitas*." Certainly the group movement was in all sorts of ways perceived as the key to any future post-war development, and not understood as a form of church renewal.

This was underlined dramatically by a German refugee pastor, Herbert Friess, whom Alan got to come and live in Frizington. Friess had been a member of the Confessing Church in Saxony, cross-examined by the Gestapo more than thirty times and preaching for five years with their agents directly under his pulpit. When he was dismissed from his job his mining congregation kept him themselves, and he continued to minister until George Bell, now Bishop of Chichester, and the person most familiar with the German scene, persuaded him to come to England. Friess later recalled his first encounter with Alan:

"We met at Whitehaven railway station. An ascetic looking priest asked me: 'Pastor Friess?' 'Yes.' He stretched out his hand and said: 'Welcome brother.' *This* made me feel at home in England and made us friends for life."

Friess addressed a large meeting in Frizington, which the Bishop also attended, at the end of April 1941, noting that it was the loss of any sense of community in the Church which had made it easy game for Hitler. Only when Hitler was already in power had the need to study the Bible and find out what it actually meant to be the community of the Church really become prominent. "When all the support the Church has had hitherto is taken away," said Friess, echoing Niemöller's famous words, "the 'new community' is found, a new 'communion' in Him who is present not as believed fact but as experienced reality." Writing from Yorkshire a fortnight later Friess commented that it was only the existence of the Church *as a body* which had any chance of resisting Fascism. "His presence has again and again and at a particular place found its incarnate expression in a body that is member and part of His incarnation", he wrote. "THERE is the only world order that will satisfy our needs. I think that is the revolution we are carrying forward in obedience. My word, what an amount of work lies before us…"

In June 1940 George Bell called a meeting of all those interested in the Anglo-German Fellowship, which Alan attended. The meeting, held at Wadham College, Oxford, brought together refugee German pastors and a good number of Anglican clergy. Alan's report, in the Carlisle diocesan gazette, shows that he had heard the distinctive emphasis of the Confessing Church, which was Barthian. The keynote is "obedience to the Word of God rather than the will of men". Nevertheless, this theology never became part of Alan's own thinking. On the contrary, his own theology always began and ended with the Church as community. "Whenever Friess speaks," Alan noted in his log book, "the question comes: What are we going to do? The answer given in Frizington is 'the group'. How are we going to START? This is the only answer to our problems, but what about the price of it?" Earlier we find this record of discussion: "Before reconstruction could begin we had to discover that the

Church is actually a Body. This situation is everywhere the same. People generally are not willing to share the responsibility and those who are willing do not know what to do." Discovering the Church as a body was not, for Alan, primarily an *ecclesiastica* problem, but a question of the future of democratic society. G. D. H. Cole's *Europe, Russia and the Future*, published at this time, and taken for study by the meeting, had an immense influence on Alan's vision of the Church. Cole argued that the 'small group' formed the essential basis for democratic life, and Alan naturally saw the parish group as the kernel of this.

In a long letter reflecting on what was going on in Frizington Gabriel Hebert summarized what he had understood. The problem, he said, is how the Church is to actualize in her life what is sacramentally given in the Parish Communion:

"Your answer was that the congregation must become a real community, of which the vicarage-house is the natural centre: the vicarage must be a community house, and therefore should not contain e.g. a drawing room, which would mark a social barrier between the priest and his people. This is the place for the group to meet: and the group will include those who are prepared to be what we once described as 'a saving remnant' in the parish, responding to the Divine call for self-giving, and abandoning the attitude of living (in heart and mind) behind their own locked front door. This was the idea *The Leap* expressed: and *The Leap* said that this was not to be for one parish only but to spread, so that Christians in neighbouring parishes should know one another as Christians. The idea behind the whole thing was largely inspired by the Confessionals in Germany, who have given it in a sense a classical expression."

In August, after an exhilarating meeting on the subject of Christian education Alan drew up a statement of the idea and purpose of the Group which ran as follows:

I. God is a "group of persons" living in perfect harmony with one another (Trinity). Human life when perfected, made and remade, in the image of God, is the life of a group living in perfect harmony, one with another. In this time, the Church must be striving to be that – to enter into that life.

II. There must therefore be, in each parish, the Church which is a group of persons living and striving to live as nearly in harmony with each other as possible, recognizing that the true centre of their lives is Christ and that this Christ is incarnate in His people as truly as He is 'before the worlds'. The centre is therefore in him and in him 'in' them and our neighbours. The Group is therefore not an organization like some sectional society but is the way in which the Church lives.

III. The Group is to be seen as the 'response' made by people becoming obedient to the call which God makes to every man. The Group can have no 'hard and fast' line of membership since men are in different stages of responding. Every baptized person is a member of the group but all are in different stages of admitting it.

IV. Upon those who do see and admit it is laid special responsibility – special ability to respond. They give more time, energy, patience, etc. to the life of the group, hearing His Word, assimilating it, confessing it.

V. In the local 'group' the parish church is the meeting place, the focus of its life. The Sacrament of Holy Community reveals the Universal World-Community in which all share, the local community which is part of the body, and the True Community which is God present. The life of the whole Church is typified in this gathering of the Church.

This vision of the Church and its role was naturally not without its problems. In the letter already mentioned Hebert turned to the inevitable criticisms, namely that the meeting tended to be élitist and to foster, if not 'holier than thou', then at least 'more righteous than thou' attitudes. He also pointed out the difficulty of giving the vicarage the central role which Alan sought to do. "In the Whitehaven Deanery the ménage of Frizington Vicarage did not in fact reproduce itself anywhere else: and it was certain that your successor would not continue it. Does not this mean that the C of E is not at present ready for just this? Or maybe that the expression of the community idea in the parish is not yet ready to take this form except in some exceptional cases...There is a transformation needed throughout the length and breadth of the Church. If we found ourselves in the situation of the German

Confessionals things would move more quickly. For the present it is vitally important that by any and every means a genuine community should be helped to grow up everywhere."

Hebert's vision was, as Wilson implied in his review, more narrowly ecclesiastical than Alan's. "The true purpose of these meetings is after all prayer," he wrote, and the extent of both Alan's agreement and disagreement with this can only become clear when we understand his later teaching on prayer. As far as Alan was concerned what was truly *sacramental* in this understanding, that is, what functioned as a sign which actually changes things, was the Church community as the effective sign of an authentic, democratic and egalitarian wider community. To be this was, he believed, exactly what the church was *for*. I was this he discovered in the course of his six years in Frizington.

When the time came for him to leave, a parishioner summed up what they had learned from him as "The worst of us can be of use." This was, of course, very much the message of 1942, but the recovery of dignity, and the centrality of the contest for full human freedom was nevertheless what the congregation felt they had taken from Alan's ministry. They had also been built more firmly into the life of the universal Church, and enabled, through Herbert Friess, to understand what was truly at stake in the struggle against Hitler. In accomplishing this Alan was perhaps no more than representative of the best parish clergy throughout Britain at the time, but to say this is in no way to minimize the achievement. In terms of an overall vision of the Church what he was struggling for was close to what Bonhoeffer was also searching for in his letters from Tegel: a renewed understanding of a community which would be at once profoundly secular, absolutely involved at the deepest possible level with the day to day lives of ordinary people, and rooted in a Christ who, as Bonhoeffer said, "is no longer the object of religion, but something quite different, really the Lord of the world."

By the time that he came to leave Alan was thirty-seven, and had been ordained eleven years. We can ask what kind of a man it was who was now emerging from the process of education, and the struggle of parish and family life. Herbert Friess described him as 'ascetic looking', and it is true that Alan cared little for luxuries – except for the luxury of books. He was affectionate, and passionately concerned for people, but never 'Hail fellow well met'. A rather fine pub lay immediately around the corner of his next vicarage, but he never darkened its doors – long talks at the bar were simply not his style. The word 'studious' could not be applied to him – he read as if his life depended on it, and indeed he believed that life did depend on 'the Word'. The Bishop spoke of him as 'contumacious', but this meant merely that he was already very clear about what Church meant, and what ecclesiastical games he was not prepared to play. He was idealistic to a fault, reflected in the upbringing of the children as much as anything else. He had no ambitions to climb in the clerical hierarchy whatsoever, though he really believed, for perhaps ten years, that *The Leap* movement was going to convert the Church of England. He had immense, restless, driving energy for the things of the Kingdom. In short, he was a man possessed by a vision.

6

LIFE IN DARNALL

We saw a stranger yesterday,
We put food in the eating place,
Drink in the drinking place,
Music in the listening place,
And with the sacred name of the Triune God
He blessed us and our House.

Rune of hospitality

Sir, the life of a parson, of a conscientious
clergyman, is not easy. I have always
considered a clergyman as the father
of a larger family than he is able to maintain.
I would rather have Chancery suits upon
my hands than the cure of souls.

SAMUEL JOHNSON

IN January 1942 Alan received a letter from Leslie Hunter, the
Bishop of Sheffield, inviting him to come and work in Darnall, in
the East End of the city, an industrial parish with a population of
ten thousand people. Hunter had met Alan at Malvern, and
been impressed by the account of the Parish Meeting he had
heard from Hebert and others. The Report of the Conference
had proposed that "where possible, the whole congregation
habitually worshipping together should regularly meet to plan
and carry out some common enterprise, however simple, for the
up-building of its community life and for the general good".
Hunter became Bishop of Sheffield just as the Second World
War broke out and, finding his diocese understaffed and
underfunded, set about a vigorous campaign of recruitment. He

wanted, moreover, to take up the Malvern proposals, and the invitation to Alan was quite specifically to start the Parish Meeting in Sheffield. George Macleod once remarked: "Leslie Hunter is not nearly as dangerous as he thinks he is." In his invitation to Alan it is doubtful whether he realized how radical the enterprise of the Parish Meeting was. Echoing Conrad Noel, Alan insisted that Christians are not reformists but revolutionaries because they believe that the present world order cannot be patched up, but must be destroyed, and a new order built on the foundations of Justice, Love and Truth. The Parish Meeting was conceived as a step on that revolutionary road. Hunter had got more than he bargained for.

Alan was to stay in Sheffield for the rest of his ministry, twenty-seven years which embraced a period of extraordinary change. When he arrived in the Spring of 1942 it was still by no means certain that Hitler would be defeated. The battle of El Alamein occurred in November of that year when, as Churchill put it, the Allies moved from surviving to conquering. 1945 saw the first Labour government, the establishment of the Welfare State, and partial nationalization. Alan's time in Sheffield took him from this period through the end of rationing, through the arrival of mass television and motoring for all, to the late sixties, *Honest to God*, the Beatles, Vietnam, and the beginning of the sexual revolution. The world which the Parish Meeting addressed in Alan's final years in Sheffield was very different from the one he met when he arrived, but it was part of the essential purpose of the Meeting to help the Church reckon with such changes.

Darnall, together with Attercliffe and Brightside, was part of the eastward spread of industry which occurred in Sheffield largely from the 1820s onwards, gathering pace after Bessemer's discovery of the air blown conversion process for steel in 1856, which precipitated the building of the huge steel concerns in this part of Sheffield: Firth, Vickers, Camell, and John Brown. Darnall lies east and slightly south of Attercliffe, separated from it by the Sheffield Canal. In Alan's day it was flanked to the north by the vast Tinsley Steel Works, with the Darnall Steel Works straddling the road at the foot of the hill near both the canal and the railway. During the week the yellow pall of smoke hanging above Brown Bayley's Works in Attercliffe completely obscured the view across the valley. Running further east was the open country of Handsworth Hill, part of the 'bright frame' of Sheffield's dark, or at least at this period, smoky and grimy, picture. Sheffield had been a centre for smelting iron and forging steel since at least the twelfth century, but it was only in the eighteenth and nineteenth centuries that it expanded to become a centre for steel and cutlery, and later for armaments, which served the whole British empire, a fact symbolized by the figure of Vulcan which surmounts the late nineteenth-century Town Hall.

At the beginning of the nineteenth century the parish of Sheffield still covered thirty-five square miles, stretching south well into Derbyshire. John Wilkinson, its Vicar for more than fifty years until his death in 1805, was a 'squarson', who lived in his own residence at Broom Hall outside the city and, like Bishop Butler, "hated nothing so much as enthusiasm". At the same time Sheffield had been a centre for Nonconformity from the time of the Commonwealth onwards (when the Vicar of the parish church supported Parliament), and there were nine chapels in the city. The politics and ethos of Old Dissent remained an important force in the city throughout the nineteenth century. This background, and Wilkinson's latitudinarianism, meant that Sheffield provided fertile soil for the Methodist revival. Wesley began preaching there in 1743 and noted forty-five years later that "the largest morning congregations I have seen in the kingdom" gathered in the city.

The Anglican Church, meanwhile, responded very slowly to the rapid growth of the city under industrialization. The Vicar had three curates to help him, one of whom served at the seventeenth century Chapel of Ease in Attercliffe. Four churches were built in the city in the 1820s in the 'Million Churches' movement, which aimed to provide churches for the growing industrial settlements, partly with a view to dampen potential revolutionary fervour and keep the masses in order. The real expansion came later, after the 1840s, when more than thirty churches were built around the city, Darnall being one. As people were brought in from outside to work in the steel works the old Nonconformist patterns changed slightly, but not to the advantage of Anglicanism – more to the process of 'dechurching' which characterized mass industrialization. The pioneer of the Sheffield Industrial Mission, Ted Wickham, noted that the Church of England could not have lost the working classes because it had never had them. The experience of the uprooting of small peasant communities, where family links often ran back into many centuries, certainly contributed to this alienation from the Church. Every parish priest in industrial England had to struggle with this problem.

To help Alan get on with the work Leslie Hunter promised him two curates, a promise honoured more in the breach than the observance. The curates with whom he began, Harry Hare, Richard Saunders, and a little later John Roebuck and Fred Clarke, all understood what Alan was seeking, and in some measure sought to continue what they had learned in Darnall in their later ministry. Things became more difficult after Alan joined the Communist Party in 1948. To have served in Darnall was to evoke suspicions in potential employers.

Moreover, Alan was a demanding vicar who expected the same rigour of fellow clergy as he demanded of himself. His acute sensitivity went together with what one of his WEA class called 'a ruthless steely quality'. The great gentleness and patience which characterized Alan's dealings with working class lay people was not always so evident in his relations with other clergy, who could find themselves withered by the intensity of his conviction. Although, as one of his curates said, he left them very much to get on with things, and treated them as equals, unspoken expectations tested their mettle. Both Alan and Delia were strong-minded and idealistic, had no time for idleness or sloppiness, and expected people to live up to what they believed. As the years went by 'the curate problem', as it was referred to in the Parish Meeting, became more difficult. Fewer curates came, they stayed for shorter periods, and they did not necessarily take away an enthusiasm for what Darnall stood for.

In some ways, though, this was as it should be. The ministry in Darnall was not that of one exceptionally gifted individual. It was a ministry of the whole community, constituted as a working group by the Parish Meeting, finding its common hearth in the vicarage kitchen. All his life Alan loathed clericalism. The

Church, the People of God, was not vicar and lay people, nor even vicar, curates and lay people but, as Paul conceived it, one community in which all had different roles and gifts.

Problems with clergy were not confined to curates. Some of them found Alan difficult because he was so clever, so well read, and so sure of his own views. An informal group which met in the early days, and included other lively clergy sympathetic to socialism such as Hedley Hodkin, Alfred Jowett and Ted Wickham, produced lively and often heated discussion. Ted Wickham joined the Sheffield Diocese in 1944, with a brief to set up the Sheffield Industrial Mission. As far as he was concerned the parish structure "presupposed a Christian conformist society" and he sought, in the passionate and ground-breaking prose of *Church and People in an Industrial City*, wholly new structures of engagement. It was a very different vision from that presupposed by Alan's insistence on the Parish Meeting and there were suspicions, doubts and hesitancies on both sides, especially as the Industrial Mission was combating Communism as one of its goals.

In April 1942, then, the Ecclestone family moved to the vicarage in Industry Road, up the hill from Attercliffe station, past steel works on both sides, past the Salvation Army Hall, the local school, the pubs and the rows of small terraced houses which constituted the parish. It was a large early eighteenth century house built when Darnall was a tiny hamlet remote from any industrial concern, noted by Pevsner as the only building of interest between Sheffield and Rotherham. When the family moved in they found it in a state of considerable disrepair. When it rained buckets had to be placed around the rooms to catch the water, and it was perpetually damp. This was to be their home, and effectively Darnall parish centre, for fourteen years. At the end of the period a number of the parishioners, increasingly worried about Delia's health, went to Ranmoor Grange as a delegation and told the Bishop he had to provide a new vicarage – which he more or less promptly did, in Mather Road, still in Darnall but slightly outside the parish boundary.

Downstairs in the old house the stone flagged kitchen, with the oven adjoining the coal fire as the main resource for cooking, and a small scullery with stone sinks for all forms of washing and cleaning, was the centre of all activities and hosted the Parish Meeting. Through this kitchen flowed a constant stream of visitors over the years, attracted by the Parish Meeting, the Party, and work for the Peace Conference. Delia had to provide for all these, and for those who wished to stay on and talk after the Parish Meeting had officially closed at 9.30. There was Sir John Pratt who resigned from his job in the Diplomatic Service over the Korean War, Joseph Needham from Cambridge, Ralph Morton from Iona, Bishop Ting from China, Albie Sachs from South Africa, Russell Chandran and Canon Biswas from India, Ilse Friedeberg from Bossey. All were provided for from the relatively meagre resources of a clerical stipend, which stretched Delia's creative talents to the limit. It appealed to her wish to live alongside the poor, and to deny herself conveniences. At the same time her artistic side, and her excellent taste, meant that the house was never squalid.

Needham and Ilse Friedeberg left vivid pictures of what it was like to visit Darnall at that time. In November 1953 Needham wrote after a visit to the parish:

"I really have never seen greater work being done than yours at Darnall, in the sphere of possibilities of a populous parish. I felt, too, as regards the atmosphere, that it resembled Thaxted as much as Oxford does Cambridge. Yet how rare it is that anything like these centres of light at Thaxted and Darnall are to be found. I was also extremely grateful for the kind and informal hospitality, including the fire in my room beside which I was enabled to fill in all spare moments, and late into the night, catching up on bio-chemical and morphological matters for my lectures. The whole visit was one which I will not soon forget."

More than twenty years later, in 1976, Ilse Friedeberg wrote to Delia, then in hospital, about her experiences thirty years earlier:

"It is now 34 years ago that you came to Darnall from Cumberland, and I had the joy of meeting you and of being completely at home in your house. For I have seldom met such an 'open' home and family – one which really belonged to all whether they were of the family or the parish or wherever they may have come from: you *always* had time for them, having finished your housework at the crack of dawn, and just being ready to be disturbed: no, not even that, for you never gave us the impression of disturbing you or your timetable, so much you were at the disposal of all and everybody, sitting down by the fire, having a kettle on the boil, and ready to listen to cares and joys, to give advice and to share.

"Your family was so open that I sometimes wondered how the children were going to take it, that their parents belonged to everybody and not to them. There is a lovely passage in Georgiou's book about his childhood in a Romanian village, as son of a parish priest. When he discovered that not only he, but everybody called his father 'Father', he was first of all very distressed that he had none 'of his own' but one he had to share with the whole of the village. However, I do not remember any similar reaction of your children. I remember the evening prayer you said before the fire: in it the people and events of the parish played a role, and it impressed me how much you were all part of it – really, the parish was a family, and the Parish Meeting expressed that."

The family in Industry Road was indeed often extended, sometimes by curates who lacked accommodation, once by an unemployed miner's family which was lodged upstairs for more than a year, sometimes by those home from overseas who needed somewhere to stay, even, in one case, to have their baby in the house! – quite apart from the endless short stay visitors. As with many homes in working class areas in those days there was no question of knocking before entering the house – local people always walked straight in.

The three boys wore clogs and hand-me-down clothes, and might be spotted sitting naked on the garden wall in summer. At first packed off to bed on Parish Meeting nights they later joined in when they had the time, came on parish trips and enjoyed the visitors – though the youngest, Jacob, once remarked, "Why can't we talk about anything except religion and politics?" Having parents who were prominent communists was not always easy, but the children supported them in their own way. When notices were torn down from the church notice board after the Warsaw conference in 1950 Giles, who intuitively related more to the Abraham side of the family, and who at this stage was the least sympathetic to his parents'

politics, went out to stand guard to see that this was no
repeated.

The family prayers of the Frizington years gave way to the
need to catch trams in the morning to get to school. Story telling
went on, as it had done for Alan himself, especially for Jacob
who was the recipient of a serial story which Alan spontaneously
invented for several years together. For holidays they went
mostly to Eskdale, and walked over the Lakeland hills, though
once the children had left home Alan and Delia managed to go
to France, and especially to Vernet in the Pyrenees, where Alan
loved to climb Carigou.

Darnall was not the easiest place to bring up a family. Jacob
was run over by a tram and only just survived. Suspicions arising
from party membership affected both the children and Delia
and conversation in local shops might freeze as she entered. On
the other hand throughout the time in Sheffield, the bulk of the
parish remained absolutely loyal. When a reporter from the
Sheffield Telegraph turned up trying to find evidence of disaffec-
tion amongst the congregation, the organist, a Tory himself
threw him out.

Though life was intense it was also full of laughter. When
Simon Phipps, later Bishop of Lincoln, turned up as an ordinand
in the course of his training, he presented his ration book to
Delia at the door. "If you think you're going to eat meat here
you've got another think coming," was her immediate response.
When he then asked whether there was any way in which he
could make himself useful she replied: "Yes, I very much need
the windows cleaning!" He proceeded to do this with such
vigour that some of the panes, held in only by grime, fell out! He
and Delia became firm friends.

On another occasion a *Daily Express* reporter stood in the
lobby directly beneath a wooden hammer and sickle, super-
imposed by a cross, which had been bequeathed to Alan by
Leonard Schiff, demanding to be shown it. When Alan got back
from his WEA class he asked her quietly whether she came as a
friend or as a reporter. When she replied, "The latter!" she was
shown the door and never did discover the offending article.
Alan was not a man of infinite jest, but he was a person of
inexhaustible, absolutely innocent, humour, able to see the

funny side of most situations, and able also to laugh at himself. Delia too, as everyone who knew her well remarked, constantly 'sent herself up' and thus ironized the Abraham family's manners and pretensions.

Ilse Friedeberg's questions about how possible it was to live such an open life was shrewd and just. The marriage was the heart of everything which was achieved in Darnall, and yet it was subject to tremendous centrifugal force. When Alan needed privacy, Delia would invite people to stay. When Delia needed time, Alan was bound up in a routine which allowed him no respite. He was no ideal husband, a fact which generated strong feelings of guilt in later years. Lear's phrase, "O, I have ta'en too little care of this," was often on his lips. Other close relationships, which Alan himself felt never touched the reality of the marriage, were not always perceived by Delia in the same way. She was often jealous and, though there were no affairs there was one relationship which, innocent as it was, wounded her deeply. There were explosive quarrels which led Alan to burn their photographs and talk of suicide – and yet what held them together was an intense mutual commitment which was not grim determination, but love, and which grew with the years. The maturing of Alan's spirituality came not alongside, nor in despite of, but *through* the marriage, so that *Yes to God,* his great book on prayer, was in a sense what the two of them had worked out together. They did not stay together because convention made it impossible to do otherwise but because, for both, this was the only way to explore the reality of love in all its depth.

The Church of Holy Trinity, Darnall, which was the focus of their ministry, was built in the 1840s as an evangelical mission church, and Alan described is as the 'ugliest church in Christendom'. Until 1920 it had been middle of the road in churchmanship, but then had a high church vicar who bounced the parish into Anglo-Catholic practices. His successor, a quiet person from Kelham, was a pacifist, which made his position in the parish difficult, and the excitement of his predecessor's time died down.

What Alan inherited in 1942 was two congregations grouped around two services, a 'Communion Service' at 8 a.m. and a 'Mass' at 10 a.m. His first task was to unite these two

congregations. By September he had managed to get one
Sunday morning service in which all were involved in every
aspect of what was going on. What he managed to do by way of
lay participation is taken for granted fifty years on, but was considered revolutionary then, although there were clergy around
the country who were attempting very similar things. Without
abandoning the Prayer Book service, Alan put intercessions in
the hands of the laity, got everyone to join in the Prayer of
Humble Access, and had the congregation bring up the bread –
which from the start was 'daily' bread rather than wafers – and
wine. The difficulty attending what now seem perfectly obvious
proposals can be seen from the fact that even the foremost
advocate of liturgical change at the time, Gabriel Hebert, was
horrified that the laity should handle the chalice. Again, Alan
asked the Bishop if one of the congregation could help in admin-
istering communion, but was refused. Eventually he got the
people who brought up bread and wine, including a woman with
a baby on her arm, to stay behind the altar and lift their arms
with his during the consecration.

Under Delia's supervision the parish made its own vestments
and frontals, as in Frizington. They managed to clear out the
chancel, take down some of the galleries, and bring the altar
forward. When the choir resisted change the parish decided to
do without one. For a number of years music was provided by a
small family consort playing pipe and fiddle, and afterwards
reverted to an organist and congregational singing. Though
Delia sang well music was not a major part of family life, and
this went equally for the church. On the other hand, Alan had
inherited his father's passion for art and the church was always
beautiful.

In 1946 the Parish Meeting drew up a list of what were
considered the major issues of the day – which included Bread
(which was rationed), Housing, Health, Education, the United
Nations, Power, and Science – and exhibitions were mounted in
church which showed through pictures, diagrams and posters,
how these were related to the Eucharist, each exhibition lasting
six months. The galleries were decorated with friezes through
the church year, or used for quotations Alan felt especially
important. The sentence from James Baldwin's *Another Country*,

Try to understand dear ones. Don't let it make you bitter, the world is bitter enough already," hung in the church for some years. Near the front of the church hung a banner in Chinese with the motto, "Truth will Triumph". For some time the Red Flag found a place in the sanctuary, as it had done in Thaxted and Sneyd. Padraic Pearse's great poem *The Fool* was on the wall, which induced the local Roman Catholic priest to come in to the church to say his prayers, feeling that here there was something to which he could relate. A young local artist did pictures of Sheffield to point up some of the things in the city that were worthy of celebration, or might be a focus of intercession. As time went on the church came to be full of art, including reproductions of pictures by Picasso and El Greco. "What strange stations of the cross," was Leslie Hunter's comment on a pastoral visit. It was in this way that Needham felt that Darnall recalled Thaxted.

Alan felt passionately about the place of children in worship, and always sought to include them, refusing to have a Christmas Midnight Mass as they could not be present. When one senior cleric came he was disturbed by seeing the children scattered round the church and organized them all in a phalanx at the front. Becoming conscious of this in the course of the service Alan stopped everything and asked them to go back and sit with their parents. Another visitor was in tears after the service, on an occasion when the children had been exceptionally boisterous, and Alan apologized, but the visitor replied, "It's because of the children I'm crying." "The chief thing," Alan wrote in September 1943, "is not to keep children quiet, but to help them to join in as fully as possible. That calls for a good deal from the older people by way of practical help, encouragement and example. Reverence in church is not a matter of noise or no noise – but much more a matter of wholehearted joining in the true spirit of thanksgiving." The point was, Alan felt, both to learn how to involve children in any piece of liturgy, but also, if one was disturbed, to learn how to offer that disturbance to God. What was taken as a distraction was in fact precisely what needed to be offered and therefore true worship.

The main liturgical innovation made at Darnall was the Baptism rite. Alan found using the 1928 Baptism service

impossible. It began, "...seeing that all men are from their birth
prone to sin...," and the moment this was said people's eye
glazed over. Together with the Parish Meeting he therefore tried
to work out what a Christian community would want to say in
Baptism. The result of a very protracted discussion began as
follows:

"Before we begin this service, may we think of what it means
This child has been born into your family. His new life came
into new surroundings. He takes his place in your home, and
you will do all you can to feed, guide and help him in the year
ahead. Here in church now, something of the same kind is to
take place. He is now going to begin a new life in the surroundings of a much bigger family – the whole family of God."

The emphasis was on explaining what was going on, very
much as the Prayer Book originally intended, "in language
understanded by the people." The order was printed and they
started to use it, making Baptism a congregational event instead
of the private affair for Sunday afternoons which was customary
at the time. About this time the Bishop told a meeting of his
clergy that they ought to be more experimental in worship. Alan
fished out a copy of the Baptism service from his pocket and
asked him to look at it. Some weeks later Hunter wrote, "I
cannot sanction the use of this," and gave five reasons why his
'brother bishops' would not agree to it. When Alan reported this
to the Parish Meeting there was uproar. For six months they
returned to the 1928 service, but it proved so unpopular the
Meeting decided they must go back to their own order. Hunter
probably knew this but he was wise enough to remain silent.

For some years every family who had a baby baptized, and all
the midwives involved, were invited to a great party, and all
their names were put up in church. As there were two hundred
baptisms a year this practice soon became unmanageable, and
had to be dropped, but by this time Baptism had been brought
firmly back into the life of the church.

The parish had a Franciscan mission in 1950, led by Brother
Kenneth, prepared for in the usual careful way in the Parish
Meeting. In their evaluation, however, people felt that what they
had learned was the ineffectiveness of missions. The Meeting
concluded that people virtually all came through personal or

pastoral contacts. "The truth is that Christian fellowship cannot be a matter of adding numbers of people to a body called Christian," Alan wrote in 1951, "but must necessarily be a matter of absorption into a body capable of giving this quality of fellowship. Its powers of absorption are therefore limited by its own standard of life." Every year nevertheless there was a 'Come Back Sunday', when the Parish was leafletted, and when people were invited to come back to church if they had lapsed. That numbers kept up over the years as well as they did was however probably less due to such efforts but to something rather different. It can be expressed in the words of one parishioner who started coming in 1943, "We were treated like royalty."

Although Alan was not interested in ecumenism for its own sake he worked hard at relations with local clergy of other denominations. There was no Roman Catholic church in Darnall, but he managed to get the local Roman priest to come and address the Parish Meeting. Christians of other denominations, including Catholics, were made welcome at the Eucharist. There were good relations with the local Methodists, after a time, and Alan was often invited to lead the Covenant Service.

Religious drama also played a big part in parish life. When he arrived Alan found that Whitsun was socially an important time, when children had new clothes, and when it was still customary for a child with a new jersey to come and ask for a penny. He therefore suggested to the Parish Meeting that they should use the Whitsun procession to signify what the church really stood for. Each year they set out to present different aspects of the life of the Church. The whole parish came to enjoy these pageants. Before the Lambeth Conference in 1958 they made three hundred banners, for all the dioceses of the Anglican communion, and carried them out into the streets of Darnall.

In this drama Pamela Keilly was of especial help. She was a professional actress who had been taken on as Religious Drama Adviser by an inter-denominational group known as 'The Association of Christian Communities'. She was able to bring vigour and professionalism to otherwise amateur productions, but in turn spoke warmly of what she experienced in Darnall. "It was here," she wrote, "I used to go for inspiration when life was being difficult. Unfailingly one got revitalized." Though the

drama in Darnall was never 'a work of art' it involved the whol
parish in a kind of act of witness. The play about St Francis, pu
together for the Franciscan Mission, was performed in the loca
park in torrential rain!

Alan's time was clearly structured. Each day he studied har
until 1 pm – preparing for WEA classes, the Parish Meeting, bu
also generally 'keeping abreast' of the latest publications in a
wide field. Theology was on the agenda, but part of a list, an
generally rather nearer the bottom. Politics, both domestic an
international, sociology, history, literature and psychology ten
ded to take priority. Each week there were at least three regula
fixtures: the Party Meeting, the Parish Meeting, and WEA
classes. Other meetings often filled what free time there was.

But from half past one until six each day he was visiting
which remained the heart of his work. There were five thousan
six hundred houses in the parish, which it took seven years to ge
round. In the course of his twenty-seven years there each hous
was visited at least three times, and he was turned away onl
once. The initial feeling of discomfort about visiting, which h
had experienced in Carlisle, never left him, but he felt on th
other hand that it was through this that he acquired whateve
knowledge of human beings he came to. The awareness of th
multiplicity of human nature, the eccentricities, disasters, hero
isms, follies, and a faint discernment of the person behind th
outworks was what it taught him. What this meant concretely i
best suggested by a few typical stories.

He knocked on one door and heard a voice saying "Come in."
He found a woman on her back on a rug in front of the fire
When she asked what it was he wanted Alan said, "Tell m
about you." She was paralyzed. Every morning her husband go
her up, washed and dressed her, and laid her on the floor. Th
neighbours came in only occasionally. This woman turned out t
be a marvellously vivacious person. Delia got her up to th
vicarage with the help of the St John's Ambulance, and laid he
on the Oxford English Dictionary. "Oh," she said, "I neve
thought I'd sit on two million words."

In a slightly better part of the parish he encountered a woma
at the door who was deaf. He found that her husband was on th
railway. They had three sons all of whom had been killed in th

war. On the news of the third she had gone stone deaf. The blow to him was different – she could talk of it and he never could. In any case he could not talk to his wife because she couldn't hear. He developed cancer of the bowels. It was at this time, in November 1950, that Alan went to the Warsaw Peace Conference. When he got back his instinct told him to go straight to the house. The woman opened the door and said "He's holding on. He wants to see you." He put out his hands, talked a little, and died. He had waited for Alan to come back.

In another house he met a woman who had been married twice. Of her first husband she said, "You know, Vicar, he was one of God's good men." Her second husband was a widower with children, and was foul mouthed in a way she detested. "I said to him 'God'll tak tha' tongue off thee one day.' So I waited. He had a stroke and couldn't speak. I went up to 't hospital an' stood at foot of bed and said 'Ah told thee Bill!'"

Another man, who had worked as a forge man in the steel works, lived in a dirty back street court and was obviously sick. As they talked it became clear that his passion in life was watching birds. In the Spring he used to get up at 3.30 or 4.00 a.m. and go to the woods around Sheffield to do this. It meant something incredibly beautiful for him. His most treasured possession was a tobacco box with some of the feathers these birds had dropped. Everything was against him and yet he had seen something of creation and its beauty and said *Yes* to it, Amen.

Adding this up from house to house Alan found somewhere or other the whole texture of human life: cruelty, ill will, festering sores, houses full of desperate tensions, but also kindness, warmth, generosity, humour, love and sharing. Why should the priest visit? One woman said: "I don't know why you come because I never come to church." The reply was: "Because I want to get to know you." Visiting, Alan felt, does not bring people to church and that is not the point anyway. He understood the purpose of his visiting to be simply to listen and to try and elicit what was going on, to make contact. Not to jockey it out with pleasant statements but, in Edwin Muir's words, "to kindle little hope in hopeless hell". What people are wanting, he felt, is the re-creation of hope in their hearts so that they can live, endure and be human. But it was just this which led one woman to say: "Well, you see, you brought God into our house."

The parish magazine, called first of all *Community* and then *New Community*, came and went with the years. When it appeared it was always of an extremely high standard. Alan noted that comparison with a news sheet produced by factory shop stewards or by the Council of Civil Liberties made most parish magazines appear quite trivial. They gave little sense that to cite Karl Barth, the Church was concerned with word "which compel men to speak at whatever cost because they find in them that which urgently and finally concerns the very marrow of human civilization." Urged to take a diocesan inset Alan refused and explained the reasons as they had been discussed in the course of the Parish Meeting:

"First of all, because we are a family to learn what good active family life is to be like, we use this paper to report on and record what is going on in the family. Articles written by eminent authorities on various subjects simply don't concern us unless they are matters to which the family is giving its attention *now*…our spiritual appetites ought not to be switched month by month from one topic to another as the editor of the 'inset' of the old parish magazine decided. Nor do we need snapshots of interesting churches in the Isle of Man to keep alive the sense of belonging to a worldwide church.

"Rather we need two things: general family news which ought to be personal – but not in any way a catalogue of names, and news of the great activity of the Church in which we share. It is important that the presentation of our Christian purpose should be such that people who encounter it see the essentials and realize that they have to reckon with them. A parish magazine made up of household hints and interesting views and a serial story confronts the world with nothing but the suggestion that the Church is playing a quiet game in a corner for those who like that kind of thing. But we believe that what we put out from the Church ought to be always in the nature of a manifesto about the life of the Church. This is a hard thing, a high standard, and we shall often fall below it. But we set that as our purpose."

Parish outings were a regular feature, but these were never treated simply as jolly 'days out'. Doubtless they were that as well, but they were meticulously prepared for, months in advance, by a study of the history of the place or area being visited, and the literature associated with it, in the Parish Meeting. The parish visited Oxford and Cambridge, the Potteries, and all the 'great houses' in the area, including the ancestral seat of Delia's family, Little Moreton Hall. In this way, too, a sense of the wider human project, rooted in local particularities, was slowly built up.

It is clear that, as the years went by, there was a certain falling off and flagging of energy. The house in Mather Road was pleasant, much easier to run, and was, of course, a centre for Party Meetings for many years, but could not be a centre for the parish in the same way as the old house in Industry Road. Aware of this, Alan investigated the possibility of moving to a parish in Cambridgeshire, in the gift of Trinity Hall, Cambridge, for the last five years of his ministry. Whilst the college was keen to present him the move was blocked by pressure from Downing Street. There was an American Air Force Base nearby and a known communist and peace campaigner was too much of a potential embarrassment.

At the same time it has to be said that, whether through making a virtue of necessity or not, he was as deeply committed to staying in a parish as he was to staying in marriage. Only through doing so, he believed, were you forced to face up to your mistakes. Further, he believed, the increasing mobility of own life meant that the pastor was required to remain, in order to foster stable relationships. "Whoever else goes, he must stay," he wrote in his last year in Sheffield. "He must stay, not bewailing the past glories and the disappearance of familiar things, but still expectant of a new theophany, still open-eyed and receptive, always rebuilding the worn fabric of personal life which it is the job of the Church to maintain."

The job of the Church is to distil from the raw, unlikely conditions of town life "perceptions which are transfiguring, redemptive, energizing, by and through the interplay of his own ministry with the work of other men. That is why he can never cease from visiting those endless rows of terraced houses ..because without this he cannot know and be known."

Parish ministry, however, was only one side of life in Darnall.

Equally important, both for the intellectual discipline it imposed
and also for an earthing in the world beyond the Church, was
his teaching for the WEA Throughout his time in Sheffield he
taught on a regular basis in the neighbourhoods of Woodseats
and Abbeydale, and, further afield, in Rotherham, Doncaster
Retford and Barnsley, travelling by bus through dark wet winter
nights, or enjoying the evening sunlight on the stone walls and
bare fields of West Yorkshire, arriving well in advance of starting
time to be available for conversation or discussion with early
arrivers. Most of the courses were on political history, current
affairs, or literature. The lectures were written out in long hand
each sentence carefully wrought and demanding close attention
After his retirement he destroyed all of these, but the student
notes for just one series make exhausting reading. A course on
contemporary literature in 1962 shows that he missed nothing
no matter how ephemeral. Books were discussed in his own
searching way, with reference to the latest literary criticisms but
not slavishly bound to it, and illuminated through the works of
Freud, Bettelheim, Steiner, Berger – the whole area of what is
now called 'theology of culture'. He was a brilliant lecturer
"Although I had attended such courses for fifteen years before
Alan came," wrote one of his class, "he was different, puzzling
and challenging." It is clear from the student notes we have that
though he was a marvellously perceptive literary critic, literature
interested him primarily because he saw it as concerned with
growth in humanness. The same was doubtless true of his
courses in history, politics and sociology, where he counted
Arthur Scargill amongst his students.

Alan always wore his clerical collar to the WEA classes, and
found in almost every case people wanted to know how what he
was teaching tied in with Christianity, or why he was a parson
when he could so easily be doing something 'more useful' or
'more interesting'. "I used to puzzle about the dog-collar," wrote
one of his Doncaster class. "He was always casually dressed and
never referred to his Church or used any theological language
For a long time I thought perhaps the 'Church' was a kind of
side line, and that he really preferred teaching or lecturing.'
This impression was cured the moment anyone visited Darnall
and found that he would be early for church services, sitting

quietly prepared, just as he was for classes, and that his skills as a teacher were evident in the Parish Meeting. Alan never imposed ideas but left people to make up their own minds about issues and to work things out in their own way, and he avoided, as far as possible, becoming a father figure. He always refused to act as a 'spiritual director' because he felt such direction was potentially damaging to the way each person needed to develop – yet his influence on the spirituality of others was both wide and profound.

In the WEA, as elsewhere, joining the Communist Party created problems. In 1948 the Vice-Chairman of the Association insisted on attending every class in his literature course, and, as a consequence of his talking about China, reported him for pushing a party line. He was called for interview, and in the following year an inspector attended the classes, but the charges were dropped.

In the Foreword to Pamela Keilly's Memoirs, which he wrote in 1985, Alan quoted John Grierson: "People must be taught to appreciate that being together, talking together, living together and working together in common undemonstrative harmony is the whole fraternity...It means that we are concerned with a multitude of ordinary things and that the very secret of them is their ordinariness." The celebration of ordinariness, which is in no sense mediocrity, so that common people could feel, as they said, like royalty, the sense that in the day to day struggle for humanness people were caught up in the drama of the redemption of the world, lies somewhere near the heart of Alan's ministry. He had, said Alan Webster, an extraordinary capacity for taking pains over things which were intensely boring. Leslie Hunter once said, in an aside, that Alan was the best priest in his diocese. In a diocese, and indeed in a Church, with more than its fair share of remarkable clergy there is no need to haggle over comparisons. But what we can understand by the remark, above all, is this redeeming of common time.

7

NURTURING THE HUMAN SOUL

I came that they might have life, and
have it in all its fulness.

John 10.10

At the risk of being misunderstood by
hotheads, I can say that our business
is more than ever in *Education*.

WILLIAM MORRIS

THE end of September 1943. By now the tide of war has turned,
and Bishop Bell is protesting, unavailingly, about Allied bombing
raids over Germany. In Britain thoughts are already turning to
reconstruction. In Darnall the Parish Meeting has already spent
weeks on the Beveridge Report, published the previous
November, outlining the provisions which will later produce the
Welfare State.

In Sheffield there is an exhibition at the Art Gallery called
'Design for Living', which is also about reconstruction in a
different way. With the children packed off to bed twenty people
gather in the Ecclestone kitchen and discuss the theme of the
exhibition with its organiser, Helen Knapp. Discussion ranges
over dishonesty in taste, our needless tolerance for bad design –
ovens we have to kneel before, sinks back-breakingly low – to the
meaning of life. The conclusion of the meeting is that we need
an education which helps us to appreciate things in use, which
will free us from the confusion fostered by profit-making mas-
querading as service to the community. Since "the way in which
we spend our leisure is an indication of what we are," the
meeting feels it is time we were roused from a passive sitting

back to manufactured amusements and set to create our own pleasures, or indeed recover those we have lost.

Mid-October 1952. The aged Churchill has been back in power for exactly one year. George VI is dead, and preparations are being made for the Coronation of Elizabeth II. Tonight twenty-five people are gathered for the Parish Meeting, including the Ecclestones' second son Giles. It is already the 524th meeting, and on a rather chilly evening Alan chairs it from a position to the left of the fire. Someone reports on the City Hall Peace Conference of two weeks previously. A long report on a meeting 'Talking Peace in Moscow' follows. Another member reports on a meeting addressed by Seretse Khama. From here to a report of a meeting addressed by George MacLeod, in which he insisted on the wholeness of life and denounced the lassitude of the Churches. At this point someone mentions Leslie Hunter's attitude to all these things, the meeting gets out of hand, and ends in uproar.

August 1957. Harold Macmillan in power, and a record number of industrial disputes. The Meeting, forty-six people tonight, is discussing various aspects of family life in five small groups. Group four looks at the role of the father in the family circle:

Answers: "The gaffer"; "The Breadwinner"; "in many families he's never in the family circle." Arthur and Phoebe thought there were a lot of fathers like this. No dissent. "Father answers the children's questions." (Mr. Brooks) "Does he?" (Chairman) Things referred to father only in an emergency. (Phoebe + general assent) Miss Fletcher quoted her own father as teaching her to be responsible and think for herself. This seemed exceptional. Reasons for fathers' passivity: "Wives try to mother him, not recognizing his proper role." (Lily Sturgess plus some agreement) "Father wants peace at any price." (Ron Whitlock) "When he gets home after working all day he wants to relax." (Chairman) This leads to howl of derision from ladies present; the men agreed.

Five years later, the thousandth meeting, held on a sunny evening in June in the Parish Hall. What the American economist J. K. Galbraith has dubbed 'the affluent society' is in full swing and, despite a growth in unemployment, it is true for most people in Britain that 'they have never had it so good'. Twenty-seven people are present for the meeting. It begins by discussing the consecration of the new Bishop, and there is then a discussion of the parish trip to Coventry, already long prepared, and of the Sutherland tapestry. From there the discussion moves on to the nature and function of liturgy. From there, finally, to the doctrine of the Trinity, in whose name the Church is dedicated.

So week by week for nearly fourteen hundred meetings the parish in Sheffield sought to understand the implications of Christian discipleship in an industrial city and in a changing world. Alan had made clear in his first week in Darnall that he had been brought to Sheffield specifically to get the Parish Meeting started. He told the Church Council that they were free to choose the night of meeting, but that after that they would continue to meet, and there would be no ending, no matter how small the numbers. The first meeting of what was, for some months, called the 'Parish Group' was held in the vicarage on 13th May 1942. It was not established without opposition. After one month the senior churchwarden came to Alan and said, 'I'm not coming to this meeting any more. It's not in the Enabling Act and we don't have to have it." Alan said: "I'm sorry, but I'll have to ask for your resignation." He never came back. Others however stayed on. People came and went, moved from the centre of the group to the periphery and back again, but the Meeting never failed, nor did it ever become a rump, or an 'in group' which excluded others. Numbers ranged from fifteen to eighty, drawing on a pool of supporters in the parish which never fell much below sixty.

Alan never dominated the meeting but 'led from behind', sitting in a low chair to one side of the fire so that he 'looked up to' the group. A moving record remains of one of the early discussions. The theme was the Transfiguration. Alan began by asking why people thought Jesus took his disciples up into the mountain.

"As we clever ones tried to think of a sensible sounding answer one of our number, a little lady of limited intelligence, but impetuous and childlike, answered eagerly and with conviction, 'To be nearer to God!' Our patronising smiles were barely concealed ..."She thinks God's in the sky." Alan, meanwhile, pondered this contribution deeply. "Yes," he said, "you mean nearer to God in the quietness?" She had sensed something of the general reaction and was becoming a little crestfallen but then immediately brightened, and beamed her approval and encouragement as Alan further pursued her idea."

The Parish Meeting was, in essence, an attempt to reconceive what it meant to be Church. It anticipated in an extraordinary way the formation in Latin America thirty years later of the *'communidades di base'*. We can see this in the description of the meeting we find in the first of two *Leap* leaflets Alan and Jim Wilson put out shortly after the move to Darnall. "The Parish Meeting," they wrote, "is simply the calling together of the worshippers, not to be addressed by a speaker, not to be a study group, not to be a 'working party', not to be any of these sectional things, but to be the Church facing its daily work and ready to find out just how it is to be tackled. Let it be understood that (this assembling) is the other half of the supreme act of worship and no less vital in our Christian life. We are not experimenting in novelties, but setting out to recover a portion of our Christian heritage which has been mislaid. We are, in fact tackling the job which underlies or precedes all plans for evangelization... The aim and value of the Parish Meeting is not to be realized in the passing of resolutions, but in the kind of change of attitude towards the life, work and membership of the Church which it brings about."

Behind the constructive proposals lay a radical critique of the Church as it was. Four major aspects of this critique were outlined at a Parish Meeting in November 1942, when the group sought to understand negative comments on the Church which had appeared recently in the press. First, they felt, the Church had failed to face the deepest problems of life, and constantly displayed a preference for building tabernacles on the mountain of vision rather than contending with problems of a humiliating kind on the plain.

Secondly, the Church for several hundred years had not preached 'total religion', religion having to do with every aspect of human life, but had concentrated on moral issues of an individual kind. The Church had become a club for the religiously minded, one leisure option amongst others, and so a sort of devotional replica of the world. It was preoccupied again and again with raising money for its own buildings, to the extent that if you knocked on a door and said you were from the Church it was assumed you were after money.

Thirdly, the Church had permitted its clergy to be recruited very largely from one social class and to be educated in one tradition or social outlook. This, together with the use of its revenues in wasteful and selfish ways, had been responsible for a huge gulf arising between clergy and people.

Finally, and relatedly, the Church had permitted social distinctions to exist inside its fellowship, and had rarely challenged these in the name of Justice and Equality. This had led quite naturally to a steady loss of corporate loyalty.

The whole critique could be summed up by saying, as Alan did in an article a few years later, that the understanding of the Church had been tampered with "to suit the purposes of worldly men". The Church had established a concordat with the world which imprisoned it in just those circumstances that its faith in the Incarnation required it to reject. The lack of connection between the world of daily life and the Church meant that the great beauty of so many of the buildings, and the dated symbolism of the liturgy, served only to reinforce a sense of nostalgia, to hem in the person endeavouring to pray in a secluded world, where the need was rather to live in a more richly disciplined imaginative way in the world outside. Such a Church had little or nothing to say to a world in crisis. J. B. Priestley had pointed out in *The Linden Tree*, a play which appeared in Sheffield and which the group studied, that in Europe people were living through a gigantic social revolution unaccompanied by secret police and concentration camps. To enable the Church to speak to this world it needed liberating. "Members of the Church can at the moment be drilled and organised," Alan wrote in 1951. "They can be taught all manner of things. But the essential relationship which it is the intention of Christ's Church to establish and embody can still be missing."

The first aspect of the task of reconstruction was the recovery of community. Alan learned from John MacMurray that "the discovery made by Jesus was that human life is personal." He added, "'Church' exists to propagate that discovery." It was and

is a truism that in industrialized society people are starved of
genuine personal relationships, badly nourished in those things
by which they come to full stature as persons. In such a situation
an enclave such as the Church had become could be nothing but
a pathetic self-deception. But the concern of the gospel, as Alan
understood it, was that people be enabled to grow to their full
capacity, and 'Church' he saw as the nurturing agency through
whose corporate concern personal life is coaxed into being and
built up in every way. "If the personal means something less
than...the mystery of God made manifest in human life," he
wrote many years later, "it is to the absence of the experience of
true community in the life of the churches and religious bodies
that this must be traced." The twin poles of the Parish Communion and the Parish Meeting were designed to foster the
creation of true community. For Alan the Parish Meeting was
not something 'the Church' *did*; it *was* Church. In a world of
atomized individualism, of mutual hatreds and antagonisms, it
existed to help people discover that we can only be truly human
in and through community. This had a political dimension as we
have seen. G. D. H. Cole had argued that democracy needed
small groups in order to survive and Alan understood 'Church'
as a federation of such groups.

"Our situation," he wrote, "is one in which the Christian
Church is called upon to show how and where people can find in
their midst a mode of living which fulfils rather than frustrates
their humanity, which takes them on as they are but transforms
them, which knows that they cannot always stand upright but
renews them, which relates them one to another in such a way as
to free them and enable them to grow up to full stature. We need
therefore to look again at the training of the Twelve, and the
pattern of the churches which came into being as the result of
the apostles' work, and to ask ourselves whether the local church
as we know it bears a recognizable relationship to those described in the title deeds. We have so often side-stepped them by
substituting a quite different conception of the Church. It is a
matter of what participation in church life does for people in
moulding and developing their attitudes towards themselves,
towards other people, towards the world and its business, which
things are an indication of their attitude towards God. This local

church must be a growing point in the context and fabric of society, a source of fermentation, a stimulus to new ventures, a provocation to surprise and exhilaration, so that those who are brought into touch with it are in some degree being transformed in mind and body...There remains with the local church the potentiality of being the instrument of human recreation, of being the nexus of all the saving powers and forces at work in the world."

Two theological key words of the immediate post war years, 'body' and 'koinonia', were taken with absolute seriousness in Darnall. What the scholars wrote about Alan sought to give flesh to "amongst the bulks of actual things". The Parish Meeting was about discovering what it meant to say that the Church was a 'body', taking Christ at his word, not turning the Word made flesh back into word again. "Men and women must recover the sense of belonging to this body by the very practical method of assembling week by week" he wrote in 1944. Such a body had as its fundamental character the recovery of the true pattern of personal life, the interpenetration of one with another, which enriches all and overrides none. Alan saw the meeting as a nurturing body, continuing what the natural family should do for children. 'Family' was a key metaphor. It expressed both the inescapability of the Christian community, the fact that Church was not a self-chosen coterie of friends, but also evoked the sense of members as children who are equally loved in spite of their differences of ability and character. Therefore, in the Meeting, Alan aimed to be as informal, intimate and homely as possible and sought surroundings which could emphasise this fact, preferring to meet in the vicarage, a family home, where the family atmosphere was already real and did not have to be created, rather than in a 'parish centre' or hall.

The class division which Alan had highlighted as one of the Church's key problems was, of course, not an immediate problem in Darnall. The parish was socially homogeneous, and though there were plenty of 'working class Tories', and even more who loathed anything to do with Communism, it was a relatively easy matter to build up a Church which was clearly on the side of the oppressed. On the other hand the 'infection' Alan hoped to spread through the Church of England was effectively quarantined. "A man who preaches both Christianity and Communism suffers from a fundamental inconsistency of mind," said Archbishop Garbett when someone complained to him about Alan's politics, and this was the view taken by the Church as a whole. The growth of the affluent society eased the difficulties of class alignment, and the nettle never had to be grasped. Both in theory and practice, however, the Parish Meeting sought to keep the issues of class distinction within the Church on the agenda and to identify it as a problem which had to be tackled.

Given this emphasis on the local community, Alan was always bound to be somewhat sceptical of Christian mission which was not based on the community. The parish was, for him, not an archaic and now outmoded structure, but a body of people drawn and held together in a spirit that prompted the members to care for, respect and love one another. It is the embodiment in any place of the I-in-You, You-in-Me relationship which Christ prayed for. Larger than the family, which has its own special intimacies and responsibilities, the parish so conceived has the job of nurturing all its members that they may, in New Testament terms, grow up to their full stature in Christ. Something begun in the life of the family is to be carried into the next necessary stage of personal development. Small enough to permit a true understanding to grow up between its members, such a body must extend their lives by confronting them with diversities of character and achievement, encouraging each and all to be themselves, relating each to a common life that is enriched by that which each supplies and yet is more than the sum of their gifts.

Discovering the body meant overcoming radical individualism. Christian living, Alan wrote, means that henceforward we are not isolated people, living to ourselves and answerable only to ourselves, but that we are members of one Body, living out our lives in and through this Body, and always both answerable to it and dependent on it. We cannot be spiritual isolationists. The meeting of those who are learning to love one another, he wrote by way of explaining the Parish Meeting, is the channel of the deepest experience of beauty and goodness that we can know, but it is a costly business to give oneself to it. No wonder then that we are tempted and persuaded to fall back upon less demanding relationships, to accept substitutes, to make do with what professes to be a true communion of persons but is not, and indeed to go all our lives without realizing we have missed the essential thing. Christianity is the intention to respond to this givenness of human nature and to work out intentionally what is necessary for its fulfilment. This amounted, he rightly insisted, to a revolution.

To suggest to Christian congregations that they should come together, not to take part in yet another church service or to join in some social function, but to realize the true nature of the Church excited, and at the end of the twentieth century still excites, surprise. And yet it was because church life had become enfeebled and cluttered up with all kinds of secondary things, all out of their proper focus, that it was not possible to make sense of the 'mystical' aspect of Christ's body. What was needed to do this was the realization that every local Church is set to be a disclosure of human possibilities, a glimpse of a brave new world disclosed through the persons of our neighbours. Alan always insisted that "Learning to love is the whole duty and opportunity of humankind."

In a discussion in the Meeting the group decided that the Church ought to differ from other groups not only in the way of joining it, in the keeping of rules, in the impossibility of winding up its affairs, but also in the fact that it was the place where grievances and misunderstandings could be faced up to and overcome. "Almost every parish is plagued by unresolved problems or hampered in its work by the necessity felt by some of keeping off certain dangerous questions," Alan wrote. "This reluctance is not seeking peace in the Christian sense at all. It is merely trying to have peace on the easiest possible terms and devitalizes the Church…The Parish Meeting becomes so much less than it ought to be if it cannot be the place where the personal problems of the Church cannot be faced. Quickness to take offence, over-impulsive retorts, personal dislikes: it is in the wear and tear of such things over the years that the quality of life of Church is tested."

The log book of the Meeting records many such incidents. In July 1952, the group is discussing reports from a conference at Swanwick on the Church and Politics.

"Discussion was pretty general over all these fields until we came to Margaret Pierrepoint's remark that 'after all this, the point was to tell people that their sins were forgiven and tell them about Jesus.' An attempt to resist this, and to show that something more in the nature of an incarnation concerned with the fuller life was involved, provoked a storm in which Conni and Sallie walked out declaring that we might as well pack up Church!"

In the hard business of learning to face up to and go through difficulties the Meeting enabled such learning. When a particularly difficult member, known for her carping criticisms, was challenged as to why she continued to come she replied simply "I come here because I know that I am loved." And Phoebe Webb, a participant of the Parish Meeting for twenty-six years of its existence, summed up its significance by saying, "It taught us how to love."

The second function of the Parish Meeting was education understood in its broadest sense as that which enables people to appreciate and play the fullest part in their world, the starting point of new efforts to set about living. "It is our contention that nothing more important confronts the Church than the task of recovering its essential character of liberating what is God given of discerning basic truths and enabling it to work like leaven again." For this task the sermon as a mode of education was clearly quite inadequate. The need was for real questions and discussion, the possibility of tussling out difficult issues. Moreover the agenda could not be set by a lectionary but was, rather, built from concern for what was happening in the contemporary world, what was given in the Christian inheritance, and what confronts us as the job of Church people. "The whole field of the moral and spiritual implications of human action in the world is ours for comment and elucidation and declaration." The job of the Church is not to help provide stock answers, the most deadly of the Church's self-deceptions, but rather to help people to see where they are in the crisis, and to begin asking questions. As a teacher, commented May Bearcroft, another long-term member of the Meeting, Alan always insisted that we must keep seeking the truth, and not to think that we had somehow got it. One visitor came to the meeting with the query: "Is this the place where you have arguments?" and the group accepted this description with humorous pride. They tried to live by Florence Allshorn's motto: "Never stop asking to be made to see. Seeing is the biggest thing in the world."

The agendas of the twenty-seven years of the Meeting show the way in which this was done. As well as discussions of congregational matters, such as the role of the choir or the rewriting of the Baptism service, or theological or spiritual matters such as praying or the role of clergy and laity, political events figured as a matter of course. No political meeting was held in Sheffield in all these years without delegates from Darnall in attendance. Nuclear power, the Bomb, Indian Independence, Suez, Hungary, China, Czechoslovakia, General Elections, local elections, all were subjects for discussion and study. Already in 1948 the group was discussing the ordination of women, and the question of gender roles crops up constantly over the years, along with broader questions of sexuality. Parochialism has its bad name, Alan commented, from the narrowness of its vision and outlook, but "the whole world came through Darnall", and there was no event of significance in all these years with which the group was not concerned.

The group went regularly to the Sheffield Playhouse, having studied the text of the play beforehand, and in this way got to know the work of Priestley, Ibsen, Robert Bolt, and Tennessee Williams as well as that of Shakespeare and Shaw. In answer to the question why this should be the Church's concern Alan replied in the words of Arthur Miller, that theatre "makes you more human, i.e. less alone."

When there were art exhibitions at the Sheffield Art Gallery the organiser was brought in to talk to the group: studies were made of Lowry, Klee, Sidney Nolan, Cézanne, Van Gogh and Picasso. For Alan it was inexcusable to talk about 'fulness of life' if all that was given to us by artists, especially by our contemporaries, was neglected. In the early days the Meeting was helped by David Hughes, a microbiologist at the University and a good artist himself, who was able to introduce the work of Klee to them when an exhibition came to the city. Although the initial reaction to his contributions was, "There's David off again," he won them over because he came consistently, and because he

was so humble minded, entirely concerned with the thing i
hand. Confronted with the incomprehension which attends s
much 'modern art' Alan insisted that one of the key tasks of th
meeting was to help people to use their imagination, to exten
their vision. It was this training which enabled the parish to loo
critically at its church building and to begin the process c
transforming it into something more expressive of a generous
concerned and celebratory attitude to life.

Again, matters of general intellectual importance were on th
agenda: Lysenko, Broadcasting, Freedom, Darwinism, novels b
Tolstoy, Sillitoe or James Baldwin, books by Teilhard d
Chardin, MacMurray and John Robinson. They read togethe
biographies of Scott Holland, Tyrrell, Bishop Gore and Conra
Noel. Newspaper articles or broadcasts were always topics fo
discussion "so that a more critical attitude may be develope
amongst us on the basis of the Christian faith." This was takin
the work of I. A. Richards into the parish, and one observer re
marked that the Parish Meeting brought ordinary people, ofte
with no formal education, up to a level of discussion worthy o
an Oxbridge college, and made inarticulate people articulate
There was a dimension of depth to this as well. Alan made yo
"grow up, stand on your own feet, and become aware of you
indebtedness to others," wrote someone who participated i
both the Meeting and the WEA classes.

Bible study was always a concern but also always one of th
most difficult areas. We need to read the Bible as the guide boo
of the Church, Alan wrote in 1942, and to see in the light of i
what the Church really is. The only possibility for a Christia
cultural revolution is a fresh look at the title deeds of our faith
Yet the Parish Meeting log books over the years chart i
continuing attempt to break through "the stilted atmospher
which envelops us every time the Bible is mentioned." Setting i
alongside contemporary literature was one way of doing this
seeing how it dovetailed into what was being said in con
temporary language. To do this, Alan insisted, presupposes i
belief in God active in the world: if we speak as if God has to b
introduced into the world it is no wonder we have problem
seeing how the Bible is to be spoken of as a pertinent book. If
like Blake, we are to find the Bible "the most instructive of al

6. *Children's play and procession, Darnall, Whitsunside, 1950s*

7. Meeting with Konni Zilliacus and Abbé Jean Boulier, 1950

8. Family farewell to Darnall, 1969, left to right, Brenda, Martin, Alan, Jacob, Delia, Margaret, Giles, Imogen and grandchildren Catherine, Richar\[d], Andrew, Joanna and Rachel

ooks" it is because like him we find it directly related to our
history.

This wide ranging agenda was sometimes a matter of negative
comment by clerical visitors. John Moorman, when Principal of
Chichester Theological College, brought a group of students to
the Meeting, and after some time remarked: "I've been sitting
here for one hour and so far no one has mentioned the word
'God'." One of the resident members turned round and said,
"Aye, and ah've had my eye on thee and tha've looked right
miserable ever since tha cam'in." It was not a difficulty felt by
the members. Phoebe Webb again summed up the parish
reaction to this extraordinary agenda: "The main thing was –
the Parish Meeting taught me such a lot."

On one level, it is true, the concern of the Parish Meeting was
profoundly and deeply secular, and yet this did not imply any
rationalist loss of faith. On the contrary, Parish Meeting, the
meeting of those who believed in and were working towards the
new community, and Parish Eucharist, were related as breathing
in and breathing out. Like the earlier Christian socialists Alan's
vision of human community was rooted in an understanding of
incarnation and sacraments, and in a profound devotion to the
Person of Christ, no mater how chary he might be of the dogmas
of Christology.

The Parish Meeting was not, of course, simply a talking shop.
Education was conceived very strictly in terms of what Paulo
Freire, working with peasants in Brazil, later formulated as
'action-reflection'. *Action* was the third aspect of its *raison d'être*,
and all sorts of involvements were entered into over the twenty-
seven years. From 1945 to 1947 German prisoners of war were
welcomed into the parish at Christmas and Easter, and friendships were established which lasted for years. Already in 1951 the
Parish was marching in protest against the hydrogen bomb. 1956
found them on the streets about Suez. Once Amnesty International was started the Parish was affiliated as a matter of
course. The meeting campaigned for safer roads in the parish,
for pedestrian crossings, for bus shelters, for better library
facilities, for the protection of the Sheffield Green Belt, and was
instrumental in founding the local Community Association
where a number of Darnall people served on its council. They

followed up questions raised at the Diocesan Conference on the subject of old age by making a survey of the parish to ascertain the numbers of old people and to acquaint themselves with some of their problems. Through the exhibitions in church they tried to show quickly and clearly to the large numbers of people who visited the church concern for the problems of the day.

When the Bishop asked what difference all his parishes made to their area Darnall was better equipped to answer than most. The meeting responded that it would rather talk in terms of the attitudes of its members to problems of common life. "We emphasise this," they said, "because we have tried to see most of these problems, however difficult, and have tried both to understand and to get clear our attitude towards them." "We have tried, e.g. to combat the prevalent notion that the Church is for ever begging or trying to raise money by various schemes, by refusing to participate in anything of the kind. It will be long before people generally realize this fact, but an increasing number know of it and appreciate it. We have, on the other hand, endeavoured to show that as a Church we are very much concerned with the promotion of community life, in a district which is conspicuously starved of the amenities of social life.. The fact of our concern for political questions is widely known and it is clear to us that these issues divide people more deeply than doctrinal, devotional or moral ones. In this respect the influence of the Church on the district is clear enough."

The meeting was the place where "the mind of the Church" was shaped preparatory to action, and where action was later reflected on. In June 1946 Alan commented on the futility of much that passed as parish work. "The very shape and attitude of the Church in the locality so often belies the scrubbing, potato-peeling, dishwashing servant of God that it should be." "Times without number it has no grasp of the job to be done, no sense of urgency about the need. Otherwise a weekly meeting of the Church, such as the Parish Meeting tries to be, would not be regarded as an 'interesting experiment', but as sheer necessity. The actual facing of the problems set by the world, the thinking and praying and planning, the sorting out of jobs and the attempt to do them, would all necessitate this continual coming together. It would be in the doing of the job that the Fellowship was experienced. It would be in the exigencies of the struggle that we found the truth of the necessity for forgiveness and Communion. It would be in the bearing of the burden that we recognized the meaning of the Breaking of the Bread. But apart from this, and so often it is obvious, we go on with an attempt to galvanize into life symbols, ceremonies, phrases which have come unstuck from realities."

Taking up the phrase of the Book of Common Prayer, the concern was for a 'militant' Church. But the Church can be militant only when its members have a clear idea of objectives, discipline, resources and tactics. This the meeting sought to provide. It was objected that people got hurt and they they could not sleep after the Meetings. This Alan saw as being in accord with the gospel descriptions of Christian discipleship. Over the years he felt they were as indebted to those who said they did not understand as to those who contributed, and he learned never to drop a comment as worthless. Again, some people came to 'have a go' at the Communist vicar, but Alan commented that these hostile visitors also played an important part because they were a reminder of the need to grow in compassion.

Though there were many visiting speakers over the years, the Meeting did not exist to give them a forum. It began from the fact that the laity were too passive, that if the Church were truly to be Church the very notion of 'laity' as those dependent on specialist trained clergy needed to change. The parson had to cease to be lawgiver, theological expert, manager, and ideal Christian, and be rediscovered as a fellow Christian, a learner as well as teacher, a servant as well as leader, taking part in the ongoing conversation which formed the Meeting. Alan himself led from behind, so that the Meeting seemed unstructured when in fact it was not. This kind of role was quite different from that of being Chairman of the Parochial Church Council. The question of the management of the Meeting tended to recur. "The difficulty of the Parish Meeting was very clearly brought out in this one," Alan noted in September 1952. "There was an immense need for the most subtle kind of steering which just didn't happen, so that we tended to flounder rather than to swim." A year later the Meeting discussed a short book Alan produced whilst on holiday and noted that "there is a danger

when the Meeting is being ably steered by a quick mind, e.g
Alan, that alterations of course were made too quickly and the
slower passengers lost their balance." What Alan aimed at i
expressed in this prayer, written on the back cover of the fina
Parish Meeting log book:

"Help me O Lord throughout this Meeting to be patient and
understanding, quick to encourage those who endeavour to
contribute, wise to elucidate and value what is said, slow to be
resentful or to make excuses in the face of criticisms, good
humoured in the face of dullness: enable me to realize through
out the meeting that this is indeed Thy body drawn together
to deepen its life; and so to deal with all its members in full
realization of this. Preserve us from all falsehoods, pride
hypocrisy, stupidity and sloth: and grant that by the guidance of
Thy Holy Spirit we may be made more serviceable to Thy
Kingdom and more responsive to Thyself – through Jesus Christ
our Lord."

The Meeting itself, discussing in Alan's absence, did not agree
with the Bishop's review of the book, in which he had written
that "another man might follow the practical advice in the book
and just not achieve the success which the author has had
because he lacks his conviction and rare gifts." They felt that the
Bishop should have added that even without the gifts it was both
possible and necessary to keep on with the Meeting. In fact the
Darnall congregation did learn a new attitude and Alan once
warned a visiting cleric: "Our people love to crunch the bones of
the clergy."

The Parish Meeting, then, was clearly not just a great venture
in adult education but more an attempt to understand the
Christian faith as a 'design for living'. Community, education
and action were what 'Church' existed for, and Parish Meeting
was Church. Alan was accordingly baffled by groups which tried
it and gave it up because it was 'too difficult'. This Meeting, he
insisted again and again, is no special organisation, but that
worshipping Body, the Church, now turning its attention to the
other aspects of its life in the world, its jobs to be done, its
membership to be known, its plans and purposes to be thought
out together. It could no more be given up than the Eucharist
could be.

"There are some things like Christian marriage and the Christian Church which can yield their proper fruits only if you are prepared to go on with them till death...an experimental approach to it is no better than an experimental liaison or a trial marriage. It is here that the sense of responsibility for the work of the Church is to be helped to grow in each person who belongs to its corporate life. It is here that that intimate knowledge of each other is to be fostered, that we may truly be members one of another. It is here that the awareness of belonging to His Body is to take flesh in our participation in the common life."

After six years of meeting he noted that "we continually find ourselves faced by elementary questions and by complete misunderstanding of what we are aiming at," and to some extent this returning to basics went on until the end. The reason for this was the temptation to turn the Meeting into something already familiar – a business meeting, a study group, or a prayer group – rather than embarking on the process of discovering something quite different. Every voyage of discovery costs much in anxiety, bewilderment, discouragement, Alan commented at the time, and exacts a great deal in tenacity, faith and hope:

"There are bound to be times when little that is exciting or interesting is being dealt with. It is there that we make our biggest departure from the kind of meeting which has an interesting speaker to enliven it. The Parish Meeting is only going to go on and take its right place in our midst if we see it, not as a means, but as an end in itself – the assembling of the Church that it may be used by God."

Of course the meeting frequently had moments of perplexity and confusion. Sometimes they might be sticky, and end in frozen silence, whilst at other times they ended in uproar. "We have survived our own dullness," he noted in 1962, after twenty years, noting the sense of strain and depression which could come over the group, the worry that after all they might be on the wrong track, but also recalling the moments of vision when "our hearts burned within us." Many times it was a question whether the meeting could survive the sharpness of disagreements between members, especially over political issues. But unity, Alan insisted, does not mean that everyone is of the same opinion. "It means that all the members of the congregation are trying to arrive at a common mind, and most concerned that their differences of opinion do not lead them to destroy the unity of the Body. The Devil wins when he persuades someone to do as Judas did, to walk out on the others and not come back. No parish church that is healthy could fail to include within itself great differences of opinion, for the Church is not a coterie of like-minded people. But equally clearly, no parish church would be anything but a failure if it pretended that these differences were not capable of being tackled in the power of the Spirit, and that the very business of the Church was to come together and hammer away at possible lines of agreement and understanding, to try to live by the faith which seeks this unity in all aspects of life." On the cover of the final log book of the Parish Meeting he wrote, "To realize the relative validity of one's convictions and yet stand for them unflinchingly is what distinguishes a civilised man from a barbarian."

From the start it was understood that the Parish Meeting was not an exclusive body, but that it was open to all who would come. It was nevertheless the danger of congregationalism which worried its detractors. Alan took note of the dangers, but believed that the Meeting was not his invention. Rather did it arise from the call to the Church to assemble itself, those who respond forming a nucleus around which others could be gathered.

The attempt to bring different parishes together, begun in Frizington, continued in Sheffield. In October 1944, in the second issue of *The Leap*, the theme was the search for new forms of society. "Quite plainly we see the way forward in the development of the local Christian congregations into closely knit communities and in the building up of a widespread common action amongst them. How far the movement towards community life inside the congregation is to go cannot be laid down. But the essential characteristics of the life are plainly spoken of in the New Testament, and it is for every Church to test itself by such a standard." The aim was to form a federation of these groups helping one another, sharing experiences, learning from one another's failures, and so making a real Christian impact upon the Church and upon the nation. "We cannot, if we believe we have God's help, aim too high." By 1946 the circulation was 550, and a conference of the groups was held in Darnall in 1947 at which Gabriel Hebert, Ted Wickham and Ernest Southcott spoke. Later in the same year a conference was held in Leeds, at which the laity were prominent. The following year however, following a conference at Queen's College, Birmingham, called by Kenneth Packard and Henry de Candole, this movement was subsumed under the *Parish and People Movement*, with its journal of the same name.

This intended to carry on the concerns of *The Leap* but in the event concentrated on the more easily attainable goals of Parish Breakfast and changing the liturgy. Great as these gains were, something both costly and vital was lost in this transition. The Meeting was after all turned into something familiar, and its critical energy defused. Its rediscovery in the form of the base communities, however, is an indication that there is something essential at stake here which cannot be so easily dismissed. Three years before retirement Alan summarized what he felt being a Christian entailed as follows: "To grow up in Christ to our full stature. We do this, as in childhood, by using all the powers in us – play and work; learning to walk, talk, create etc; learning to deal with friction, faults, mistakes; learning to SEE the objective character – the truth of things – and to live in the real world by action; learning to co-operate with the changing world – to help it on; learning to wonder at and admire and enjoy the real world; learning to do this in full communion." All this was the agenda of the Parish Meeting and through it was created a Church truly in, but not of, the world.

8
THE PARTY

Blessed are those who hunger and thirst after
righteousness.

Matthew 5.6

As the parson has ever gone hand in hand with
the landlord, so has Clerical Socialism with
Feudal Socialism...Christian Socialism is but
the holy water with which the priest
consecrates the heart burnings of the aristocrat.

KARL MARX

THE Labour Party fought the first General Election after the
War on a six-point programme: economic expansion along with
price and rent control; public ownership of the Bank of England
and major industries; full employment and the repeal of
restrictive Trades Union legislation; investment in housing; full
implementation of the 1944 Education Act; and the preservation
of peace. From the perspective of the end of the century, when
so much accomplished by this administration is under threat or
has been repealed, it is what was achieved of all this that stands
out. At the time, however, there was widespread dissatisfaction
amongst Socialists about the failure to implement this programme, even though the Labour administration contained
genuine left-wingers like Stafford Cripps and Aneurin Bevan.
Many felt the Labour Party had already abandoned a full-
blooded commitment to socialism. Although India and Burma
were granted independence, colonial policies were still pursued
in Egypt, Malaysia and Indonesia. In Greece a puppet right-
wing government was installed in the teeth of popular resistance.

Ernest Bevin told the House of Commons in 1946, "I am not prepared to sacrifice the British Empire because I know that if the British Empire fell...it would mean that the standard of life of our constituents would fall considerably." In defence policy the government opted to join the nuclear club, and allowed itself to be co-opted into the Cold War by the American administration. On the home front nationalization left eighty per cent of industry in private hands, and the urgent need to build new homes moved more slowly than it had done in the period between the wars. The disparity between wages and prices led to a rapid increase in strike action, eventually met by calling in the army to man the docks.

It is hardly surprising therefore that between June 1947 and May 1948 nearly five thousand people joined the Communist Party, which had otherwise suffered a sharp decline in numbers from a peak of 66000 in 1943. Alan and Delia were part of this movement, Alan joining in February 1948, followed by Delia a week later. "I joined," he wrote later, "because I believed that the British Labour Party had by that time made it clear that its concern for Socialism at home and abroad was quite dead. Internationally it was patently anti-communist; at home it had ceased to be able to will the transformation of society towards Socialism. The Communist Party alone was wholly committed to that cause." What the cause meant he explained in a manifesto to prospective voters nearly twenty years later:

"The Communist Party alone takes Socialism seriously and proposes to end the exploitation of man by man, and to promote a society in which each will contribute according to his ability and receive according to his needs. To give what help I can to the furtherance of such aims seems to me to be a matter of duty."

Alan was never a doctrinaire Marxist. He came to Marxism from the Catholic Crusade, from William Morris, and above all from John MacMurray, who made clear the connection between Community, Communion and Communism, and for whom the study of Communism was a necessary prelude to the understanding of Christianity.

What Marx meant to him he set out most clearly in a brilliant lecture to Sheffield University Catholic Society in 1968. In this

e anticipated much of what Liberation Theology had to say in
he following decade. Marxism he understood as a practice, but
practice born of intelligent analysis. He rejected the distinction,
hen fashionable, between the early and the later Marx. From
rst to last, he believed, Marx was fundamentally concerned
vith the problem of how to be human, and therefore with
uman freedom. Alan regarded him as 'the greatest of all
umanists' in virtue of his all-round concern for everything
uman. What attracted him was the way Marx brought philo-
ophy, history, economics, and everything else which touches
uman life to the human judgment seat, to make all things
eveal what they did to and for actual human beings. Socialism
neant for him the attempt to use all resources to enable all
uman life to be fulfilled, the recognition in practice that nothing
uman must ever be handled in a contemptuous way.

Marx he regarded as a kind of prophet, whose principal work
vas the liberation of human beings from the illusions fostered
nd passed on to them. People who engage in the discerning of
ruth in human situations and demand that people face the truth
y taking sides, by changing behaviour, by reshaping their
ehaviour, are prophets akin. Marx demands that we see the
Son of Man in the hired labourer and the poor of the earth.
Without Marx, but not claiming everything for Marx, he main-
ained that the achievement of a world society within which a
new presentation of a Catholic form of Christian faith could
perate was not possible. He understood perfectly well that
Marx was not a moralist, sitting in judgement on individual
apitalists, but one who strove to 'shorten and lessen the birth
pangs' of the new world. The attraction of Marx was never-
heless fundamentally moral: what attracted Alan to him was his
protest at treating people in an inhuman way, as 'hands', as
appendages to the machine'.

Two years before Alan joined the party Karl Popper pub-
ished *The Open Society and its Enemies*, which accused Marx,
along with Plato and Hegel, of holding a determinist philosophy
of history. Alan never accepted this accusation. What Popper
drew attention to, in his view, was simply the fact that human
actions had necessary consequences, and that we could therefore
set intelligently about them – not that they were predetermined

by economic circumstance. Alan appreciated Marx's refusal to have any truck with abstraction. In turning away from abstraction he brings us into the field of the personal, into those relationships which transcend the dualism of mind and matter, spirit and body, individual and society. Part of Marxism' 'necessary work', Alan believed, was the destruction of the idealism which has passed for Christianity.

Alan's decision to join the Party remained firm, even though he lived in an area of Yorkshire where the Labour Party was efficient. Apart from one brief interlude it had run Sheffield for more than a generation. Alan had the highest respect for many of its representatives, who helped him over the years in all sorts of ways. When the Economic League was feeding anti communist literature to the Grammar School, for instance, they quickly got this stopped, and they responded to all the Parish Meeting campaigns for road safety devices and for the community centre. Alan nevertheless believed that it was important to take up the struggle for a more thoroughgoing socialist initiative. Belonging to a party was simply one way of sharing in political life, showing publicly where one stood, and giving a person the opportunity to learn from and contribute to shaping the outlook and life of the community.

No difficulties were placed in the way of his joining. Membership of the Party was open to any "who are prepared to work for the achievement of socialism", and its aims and constitution proposed no religious test. Its party programme declared that "freedom of religious worship needs to be guaranteed and all religions, creeds and beliefs respected". Only in one respect was he unable to satisfy the usual requirements for membership: he could not join a union!

For the next twenty-one years Alan and Delia attended branch meetings on Monday night, which as time went by came to be held in the vicarage, along with study weekends on various issues. Prominent Party members like Willie Gallagher, MP for Dundee, Harry Pollitt, Jack Dunman and James Klugman were all guests at the vicarage, as well as the Soviet Deputy Minister for Education. Membership of the party was always small, which meant that big demands were made on its members, and Alan learned much from the devoted self-effacing work others gave it.

Both Alan and Delia played their full part as party members: selling pamphlets and *The Daily Worker* on the streets, taking part in public demonstrations, and, increasingly, speaking at public meetings. As one of the best informed and most committed local members Alan got through the whole of West Yorkshire, speaking in Bradford, Leeds, Halifax and other towns. Such meetings did not exactly conform to the caricature of the revolutionary haranguing great crowds with a clenched fist. When asked to go to the Brightside constituency to talk on the party's policy on education only two pensioners turned up. Alan solemnly addressed them, and the party agent said it was a very good meeting! At Dronfield he gave a talk on *The German Ideology* and the members asked, "What on earth do you want to talk about that for?"

Sheffield was the stronghold of the Engineering Unions, eight or nine of whose thirty-six branches in Sheffield were Communist led. He was frequently asked to talk at branch meetings and, as Bert Ramelson, the Party Secretary for Yorkshire, put it, they were all very proud of him. Just occasionally there were flashes of anti-clerical sentiment, especially in the early years. One night in a meeting a member intervened before Alan spoke. "Mr Chairman, Point of Order. I move that the speaker be not heard." There was a solemn vote, after which Alan was allowed to proceed. At another meeting Alan was putting questions to a visiting speaker who said to him: "Tell me, comrade, what do you do?" For reply Alan just pulled his scarf away to reveal his dog collar. "O God," said the speaker, "I thought you had an intelligent face!"

More characteristic were the meetings where Alan was asked to speak about his faith. At one meeting when he was set to speak on the Peace Movement a member intervened with, "Comrade Chairman, I move that we overlook standing orders so that our brother here can talk about God," thus waiving the rule that they were not to discuss religion. Nonplussed at first, Alan's Catholic Crusade training stood him in good stead, and he talked about the Old Testament prophets and the God they were proclaiming. The chairman, an old Yorkshireman, concluded the meeting, "Well comrades, ah reckon we'll have to go 'ome and open olt book."

Alan always felt that the party reminded him of nothing s
much as the Church of England. New members were expecte
to attend instruction which was a sort of Confirmation class and
Alan felt, as remote from life as these usually are. The concer
was to get the doctrine right, and the contribution to thinkin
and acting was nil. "Almost all the 'kinds' of people recognizabl
in a Church were to be found there – almost all the typical res
ponses and attitudes to attendance, jobs, personal feeling
etc…You notice the claptrap – either of dogmatic utterance.
solemnly expressed as if they solved all the problems…or of th
idealistic pie in the sky kind that doesn't nourish hope but puts
smoke screen round the realities. You notice the ways in whic.
people respond – those who take on jobs, those who don't, thos
who are overloaded…those who play a part. You notice how
much or how little inquiry to ascertain truth goes on – how
formulae provide ways of escape from self-criticism, how piou
aspirations do duty for genuine confession." The hierarchy in
King Street also bore more than a little resemblance to th
episcopal bench!

Alan and Delia stayed in the party through some of its mos
difficult years, in particular through the exodus of the intellec
tuals in 1956 over Hungary, and later in 1968 over Czecho
slovakia. As opposed to the 'Moscow Line' orthodoxy of part
headquarters in King Street local branches were able to be
much more critical. When a party speaker came up from
London to give the official line on Malaya, E. P. Thompson
came down from Leeds and sat in the front row interjecting
"Liar!" at every point that was made. About the same time
shortly after the Ecclestones had joined, another crisis arose
when criticisms of the Stalinist geneticist Lysenko, who em
phasised environmental influence on heredity, came to the fore
J. B. S. Haldane, the most prominent scientist in the Party, with
drew from active work when *The Daily Worker* published article
in support of Lysenko and refused to publish his criticisms. An
aggregate was held in Sheffield, when all members were sup
posed to attend, and the microbiologist David Hughes, who wa
also a member of the Parish Meeting, left the Party at this time
When Hungary came along it was traumatic. An aggregate wa
called which met every night of the week. Many prominent

intellectuals left at this time, but Delia and Alan decided to stay in, not to endorse what had happened but to work out what to do. They took the line that the commitment they had made meant it was improper to withdraw when things were difficult, and Alan always felt that party membership enabled him to look at the political situation from the standpoint of the obscure person in the street.

Fellow clergy felt that Alan defended Stalin far too forthrightly, but within the party Alan challenged the attitude to Trotsky and got the branch to study the *Testament of Lenin*. When Ramelson came to take charge of the discussion over Czechoslovakia he began to give the party line and was told firmly: "You keep quiet!" When the Electricians' Union was convicted of ballot rigging they had a branch meeting immediately afterwards. Delia condemned it and spoke of the need for honesty, and the Secretary asked testily, "What good would that have done?" Delia replied, "You wouldn't have been found out, would you?"

Though few members of the party were practitioners of any religion, Alan's priestly function was recognized on a number of occasions when he was asked to take funerals for party members. He did so, not as a priest, but as a fellow member who had something worthwhile to say in the face of death. He spoke at the graveside of the concern for what it is to be human and on the text of John Ball, the priest who led the Peasants' Revolt: "Fellowship is heaven, lack of fellowship is hell." Words he used then were used at his own funeral, "This fragile life between birth and death can nevertheless be a fulfilment – if it is a dialogue. In our life and experience we are addressed; by thought, speech and action, by producing and influencing we are able to answer." (1)

After one such service the widow of a Leeds Communist wrote, "That's exactly what my husband and I would have wanted." Membership of the party certainly put him in touch with those who were right outside the Church and who had no time for it.

It was above all involvement in the Peace Movement which drew Alan to the Party in the first place, and in which he played a prominent part. Churchill's famous 'Iron Curtain' speech was

made in America in March 1946. By March 1948 Ernest Bevin
was already expressing government support for the Atlantic Pact
now known as NATO (concluded in April 1949). The introduction of a new currency in the Western-held zones of Germany
prompted Moscow to close all communication with the Eastern
zones, and the Berlin airlift began. Attlee defended the stationing
of American planes in Britain for this exercise by saying that the
Western governments expected the Russians to "sweep right
across Europe".

In the face of this acute tension a joint French-Polish Committee for Peace called a 'World Conference of Intellectuals for
Peace' in August 1948, in Wroclaw in Poland, which drew
together people from forty countries. From Britain the delegation included Julian Huxley, J. B. S. Haldane, Ritchie Calder,
Christopher Hill, A. J. P. Taylor and the Dean of Canterbury
Hewlett Johnson. Taylor, who had flirted with Communism as
an undergraduate but had been disenchanted by the party line
on the General Strike, was one of the twelve who eventually
dissented from the resolution worked out by the Conference. He
disagreed with a motion which condemned only American imperialism and promised that "whatever statement is manufactured
I shall vote against it". His claim that he "wrecked the unanimity
of the Conference" is however hardly borne out by the fact that
it was signed by 423 of the delegates.

An International Coordinating Committee for Peace was
established which called the First World Peace Congress in a
still devastated Paris in April 1949. Two thousand delegates
attended, and Alan and Delia were amongst the British
representatives, along with the Labour MP Konni Zilliacus. Alan
had heard about the meeting through the party, but wrote to
Stanley Evans in Dalston, who was Chairman of the Society of
Socialist Clergy, and asked if he could go as a representative of
the Christian Socialist Movement. Alan and Delia's movements
were closely monitored by British Security, their hotel room
receiving constant anonymous telephone calls. Coming back
slightly earlier than Delia, Alan was questioned at Customs
about her whereabouts when there was nothing on his passport
to indicate he was even married.

Sartre spoke at the meeting, and Alan had the chance to meet

9. *At Stalinabad, Tadjikistan, May* 1955

10. *Tashkent, Uzbekistan,* 1955, *with the Grand Mufti of Central Asia*

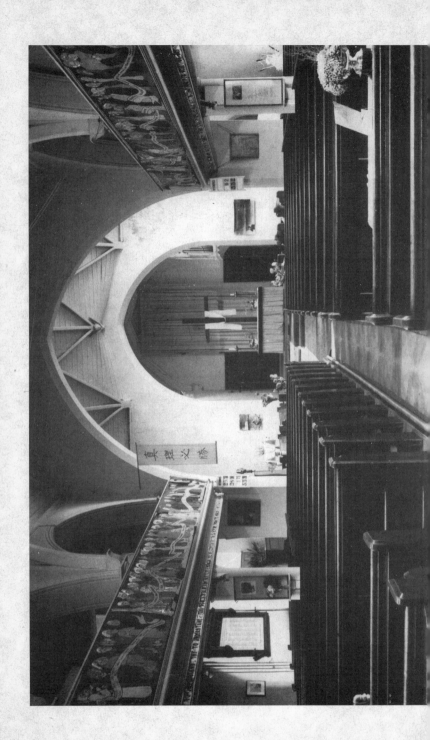

修之理真

he Abbé Boulier, whom he got to come to Sheffield and address
he local meeting of the Peace Council in 1950, before he was
unfrocked by the Vatican on account of his left-wing sympathies.
n the course of the proceedings the Christians got together. As a
Swiss pastor started talking, another Christian Socialist delegate,
Edwin Charles, remarked, "This is where the counter-revolution
begins." In fact it was precisely at this time that Barth was
making himself deeply unpopular in Basel by refusing to go
along with anti-communist sentiments and by supporting the
Czech theologian Josef Hromadka in Prague.

From this meeting sprang the World Council for Peace which,
like the earlier Peace Pledge Union, collected signatures – 473
million worldwide – for peace and against the possession or use
of atomic weapons. In Britain a committee based in London
coordinated activities nationally, but local committees looked
after events in their own areas, and Alan was Chairman of the
Sheffield Peace Committee. In this capacity he spoke at meetings
in many of the northern universities and organised monthly
meetings at which, amongst others, Boulier and Zilliacus spoke.
In addition fifty thousand signatures were collected in Sheffield
for the Stockholm Peace Petition and this level of activity led the
central committee in London to propose that the second World
Peace Conference should be held in the city in November 1950.
The local Labour Party was at first behind it. The Government
was apprised, and Attlee promised that only delegates with a
specific charge against them would be excluded. In Sheffield the
Town Hall was booked and arrangements began to be made
for the Conference, which was to open on Monday, 13th
November.

As the event drew nearer however the authorities got cold
feet. The Korean War was at its height, and critics of the
Government, like Monica Felton, were on the verge of being
accused of high treason. In October the British Council of
Churches refused to send representatives and Bishop Bell
denounced the movement as a trap and an instrument of
Cominform propaganda. On 1st November Attlee likewise
denounced the Congress as 'bogus' and a 'camouflage' for Communist propaganda. At the very last moment, on 10th
November, the Home Secretary, Chuter Ede, refused visas for

two-thirds of the two thousand delegates, for reasons which are
still unexplained. The relevant file, PR 87, is still embargoed in
the Foreign Office. Amongst those who turned out to be
'persona non grata' were Shostakovitch, Pablo Neruda, Paul
Robeson, Metropolitan Nikolai, the head of the Russian
Orthodox Church, and Frederic Joliot Curie, the President of
the Peace Movement.

In Sheffield the local press carried a somewhat hysterical
account of the whole affair, and the big steel firms refused
permission for their workers to attend, in despite of which four
and a half thousand people turned up for the opening day
which Alan chaired. Hewlett Johnson was amongst the speakers
but the star was Pablo Picasso who spoke in Spanish with
simultaneous translation:

"Dear Friends, you will allow me at the opening of this
magnificent meeting to recall a personal memory. My father
who lived in Barcelona, was an animal painter. He loved to
depict birds and particularly doves. As his life was waning, he
began to allow me to use his paint brushes, and used to ask me
to paint in the feet of the doves for him, a very delicate work
which he could no longer do. When he found I could do it fairly
well, he gave his paint brushes to me and I have succeeded him
in the family of painters. What joy he would feel if he were still
alive to see that my so humble doves have circled the world. In
this way I have contributed, with my powers and with the same
conviction which I have put into my art, to the struggle for the
first and most just of all causes. I am for life against death, for
peace against war."

With that he drew a dove which was immediately auctioned
for £21 to help raise funds for the Peace Movement. He was
asked to attend an exhibition of his art then showing in London
but declined on account of the British Government's attitude. It
was indeed dismally McCarthyite behaviour for a Labour
administration. On Thursday all the delegates flew to Warsaw
where the conference went ahead, Alan and his curate, John
Roebuck, going as delegates, along with a member of the Amal
gamated Engineering Union.

Two years later, in December 1952, the third World Peace
Conference was held in Vienna, and Alan was again invited to

go as a delegate. Immediately prior to it he was asked to accompany Ann George on a visit to Bucharest, but heavy snow detained them in Budapest, where they were warmly received by both student and union groups. From Budapest they were able to travel to Vienna where, amongst the two thousand delegates, he met the Czech theologian Josef Hromadka, for whom he retained a lifelong admiration. Hromadka pioneered what later came to be called 'Christian-Marxist dialogue', writing in May 1948 that "Communism is partly heir of the age-long craving for social justice and equality, partly the child of the errors, blindness and greediness of the decadent bourgeois society." A pastor from Hromadka's Church, Frank Hnik, visited Britain shortly afterwards, and insisted that, for the Czech Protestant Church, "the victory of Socialism and Communism belongs to the plan of the Almighty Father…We are not afraid of the future of Christianity in the new Socialist landscape." Like Alan this was because he and Hromadka understood Socialism as the attempt to create "the realm of liberated work, of freedom from exploitation, of social justice and of real brotherhood between the nations." Socialist humanism and the Kingdom of God were not confused, but an analogy between the goals of both was posited.

Coming back by plane the English group met the Vietnamese delegation at Zurich, arriving late and bitterly disappointed that they had missed the proceedings. Alan told them that the Dean of Canterbury was in their party, and asked if they would like to meet him. Their eyes brightened and Hewlett Johnson spared them nothing. By the time he had finished they felt their trip had been worthwhile and the 'Red Dean' appeared to be their best friend in the world.

Alan did not attend the fourth World Conference, which was held in Helsinki, but he did continue peace activities in Sheffield. In January 1958 Konni Zilliacus addressed a day conference on nuclear weapons in Brook Hill in Sheffield, and out of this emerged a plan for a protest march to be held in April and for a collection of signatures to be made. A quarter of the one hundred marchers came from Darnall parish, and the church cross was carried. Unfortunately Alan had forgotten to inform the police and they stopped the march and arrested him. The Party was all for a fight, and were relishing the prospect of the police

pressing charges, but these were dropped. The Chief Constable
may have contacted Leslie Hunter and been told that Alan was
'harmless'. *The Sheffield Telegraph* carried an anti-appeasement
style editorial, "In whose name did they sign?" and Alan replied
with a passionate defence which, to the credit of the paper, they
printed:

"First in the name of Him to whose crucifixion you devoted
half of page four and forgot on page six; in the name of The
Lord *The Giver of Life*; in the name of the World Council o
Churches; in the name of innumerable great Christian leaders
including Dr Schweitzer, Dr Niemöller, and George Macleod; in
the name of the victims of Hiroshima and Nagasaki; in the name
of our congregations; and 'in the name of reason and
conscience, our own and others, which cry out against the folly
of planned annihilation' ."

Alan twice went on party delegations to Eastern Block coun
tries. In 1950 he was included in a Trades Union delegation to
Czechoslovakia. In June 1955, a year before Kruschev's famous
denunciation of Stalin, he was asked to lead a delegation to
Russia. The group included a woman lecturer at Birmingham
University who was a fluent Russian speaker and one delegate
from the National Union of Railwaymen.

In Moscow they were asked where they wanted to go, and
Alan named Tadjikistan. Their hosts were a bit taken aback, but
accepted the reason given – namely that since Britain had been a
colonialist power, and Tsarist Russia had treated these areas as
colonies, they wanted to see what Soviet Russia had made of
them. So it was arranged that the group would leave Moscow in
four days time.

In the meantime they were taken to one of the cathedrals and
introduced to Orthodox priests, and to a synagogue, which was
full. They asked to go to an ordinary Court of Justice, and sa
through a morning at a Magistrate's Court, where two cases of
embezzlement were being tried, one of which involved a party
member. The group tried to be critical, to an extent which made
one Stalinist member of the delegation angry. When the
railwayman put questions about what a train driver was paid
they were met with the answer: A Soviet train driver can earn so
much. As an experienced union man he was only too used to this

kind of language and replied, "I'm not interested in what he can earn, but what he *does* earn." But the university lecturer intervened: "It's no use going on. They won't tell you." They met the Moscow City Soviet, which predictably glorified achievements in Moscow, and the Deputy Minister for Education, who had visited the Ecclestone house in Darnall. Here, too, questions were evaded. One of the group asked what provision was made for spastic children and the question was never answered. It recalled only too painfully Laurens van der Post's experience when he asked about facilities for left-handed children: he was told there were no such children.

They stayed for some time in Tashkent, half of which was rebuilt and the other half of which seemed to consist of mud huts. They visited a Jewish community there and one member remarked, "They're frightened to death." At the same time the group were being shown extraordinary things which were clearly a great achievement. The trip also had its lighter moments. At the Opera House in Tashkent they saw *The Hunchback of Notre Dame* and they were later entertained by the Grand Mufti of Central Asia where, as it was Alan's birthday, he was dressed up in Uzbek costume!

Were Alan and his fellow Communists at the time culpably naive? They suspected the existence of the Gulag, though not at all to the extent it was soon proved to have. Alan noted in a paper in 1967 that, "In the defence of a minority position the garrison mentality tends to become second nature and it is all too easy to defend the indefensible." He acknowledged frankly that he had neither acted nor spoken nor thought wisely on innumerable occasions in the working out of the consequences of the decision to join the Party. Like the Webbs twenty years before he was doubtless deceived by some of what he was shown. Nevertheless he continued to believe in the possibility of the deliberate construction of a home for the human family which would draw upon every kind of scientific and imaginative resource and it was this socialist dream he refused to surrender.

His activity for the Party led to the proposal that he should stand as a parliamentary candidate, but this never materialized. He did however stand as a municipal candidate five times, commencing in March 1962. This triggered a great deal of press comment both locally and nationally, as it was the first time a clergyman had stood for the Party. One or two other clergy joined the Party, but never made this public. Other prominent left wingers, like Hewlett Johnson and Stanley Evans, never joined. Alan was selected as a candidate, not to take advantage of his position as a clergyman, but, as the agent put it, because "we consider him one of the foremost and best informed members of our Party in this area." Wide press coverage produced a good deal of hate mail, and abusive telephone calls. One person wanted Canon Law amended so that membership of the Communist Party would deprive a person of Orders. Others read him lectures on materialism and Stalinist persecution. "It would be interesting to know what kind of sermons the Revd Alan Ecclestone preaches," wrote one person to *The Sheffield Telegraph.* "Does he tell his people, 'Seek ye first the Kingdom of God' or, 'Seek ye first the Kingdom of Communism'?" She obviously never bothered to find out.

More interesting were the people who wrote in support from all over the country, mostly very inarticulate, many of them pensioners, expressing a long felt need for Christianity and Communism to be seen together. William Brayford, a hairdresser in Stoke, sent a postal order for 4s. with the message "1000 congratulations for sheer courage." 'Two Non-Religious Christians' sent a £5 note. A First World War veteran, disabled and unable to work, wrote from Cheshire. "There is nothing I would like better than to shake you by the hand." An old lady who had been born and brought up in Darnall wrote, "Oh, what spirit and daring, I do admire you!" Another 74-year-old widow sent "a small contribution to expenses". Letters came in from other Communist Christians around the country saying how much his stand meant to them: "I can't describe how grateful I am and how much stronger I feel somehow."

In reply to his critics Alan reminded those who brought up Stalinist persecutions that "Christians persecuted cruelly and wickedly as long as they had the power to do so," and that the shrill linking of atheism and immorality overlooked the reality of non-Christian Britain. What he had found among Communists he said, was "a passionate concern for the building of a better order of society where privilege shall give place to equality of

rights, for the redressing of ancient wrongs, and for the establishment of the fullest human life for all men and women."
"Because as a Christian I believe in and want these things established in our country," he went on, "I am proud and glad to be
associated with them." To the charge that Christianity and
Communism were incompatible he replied that the real alternative to Communism was Capitalism, which he regarded as the
true menace to the world.

Alan canvassed in his dog collar, meeting the amused tolerance which English people extend to Anglican clergy who do
other than support the status quo. One man took hold of the
election manifesto by its extreme corner, like a dirty rag, and
said, "Cum 'ere, ah'll show thee what ah think of thy ideas,"
walked through the house, and dropped it in the dustbin! In the
event Alan came bottom of the poll with three hundred and
thirteen votes. This was raised to just over three hundred and
fifty the following year, but dropped to one hundred and sixty-
five by 1966, by which time he felt it was time to call it a day.
At a Confirmation after one of these elections Leslie Hunter
sidled up to him and said: "I suppose your head is bloody but
unbowed!"

That remark of the Bishop marked the end of a very long
period when Alan had been cut off. The Church authorities
were far less comfortable with a Communist priest than Party
Headquarters were. When asked for his opinion of Alan's move
in 1948 Garbett, the Archbishop of York, replied that it was
'illogical', which was a fairly standard reply. Communism was
identified with philosophical materialism without remainder. To
be both a Communist and a believer seemed to many quite
impossible. Hunter wrote and warned Alan when he joined the
Party that he was going to make it very difficult for his fellow
clergy. All left-wing clergy were liable to experience this difficulty. Hewlett Johnson was treated with icy courtesy by Archbishop Fisher and the staff of Canterbury Cathedral, and when
Alan went to preach for him he received the same treatment.

In Sheffield the Bishop was under pressure from establishment
members of his own diocesan committee to 'deal' with Alan, and
a large file of complaints and reports, some from the highest
quarter, accumulated. This meant that, although an intensely

conscientious priest with a 'Double First' from Cambridge and
wide experience might have expected preferment, or at least a
canonry, this was impossible. It was felt that Alan had defended
Stalin too publicly to make this possible. When the Peace Conference was being organised Alan was incautious enough to tell
the Press that the Bishop had asked to be 'kept in touch', and
this provoked a furious reaction. When John Roebuck accompanied Alan to Warsaw, Hunter wrote him a stinging letter,
threatening to remove his licence. On return Alan wrote an
equally passionate letter back and sent it up post haste to
Ranmoor Grange by the hand of Giles. Back came the reply:
"You have told me all my faults. Now come and talk with me."
When a diocesan training scheme was established at Whirlow
Grange in 1953 Alan was at first not invited to join in, though he
later became one of the principal participants.

However, when the Cold War thawed, Leslie thawed. He
once took Alan by the arm and said, "I don't get any complaints
from *inside* the parish." Amongst the local clergy one pursued
him in the Press, but many others, whilst not agreeing with his
politics, were sympathetic and had him to preach. In the parish
no such difficulty was encountered. Alan told his congregation
that he had joined the party the first Sunday after having done
so, and said he would not mention it again, a promise he
honoured. He did not 'preach Communism', though peace and
justice themes were prominent enough. Seven members of the
parish finally followed him in to the party, though not all stayed
for as long as he did, and he never asked people to join – rather
the reverse. There were no mass walk outs and, as already noted,
the congregation was intensely loyal in the face of press
harassment.

After the opening of the Second Vatican Council in October
1962, Christian-Marxist dialogue, long a reality in Eastern Bloc
countries, began to get under way in Britain. *Marxism Today* ran
an issue on the dialogue in 1966, and discussion continued for a
full year. Alan was naturally included on both sides of this
debate from the beginning, contributing to *Marxism Today* as a
Christian, and to local debates with Christian ministers of all
denominations as a Communist. The work of Teilhard de
Chardin was providing a meeting point for Christians and Com-

munists at this time, and Alan led courses in the diocese on his thought. Prominent members of the Party attended the Teilhard Conference in London in 1966 addressed by, amongst others, Roger Garaudy. Teilhard's rooting in science, and his emphasis on human potential was what attracted non-Christian Marxists, whilst Alan was attracted by his concept of the 'theosphere' constantly bearing upon us.

In October 1967 a Marxist-Christian conference was held at St Katharine's, Stepney, under the title *What Sort of Revolution?*, and Alan chaired the press conference at its close. In December of the same year Alan sat on the Communist side of the panel in a discussion of 'The Marxist and Christian Concept of Man'. Whilst discussion was wide ranging, the particular focus was on racism, and a joint Christian-Communist initiative to combat racism in Yorkshire emerged at the beginning of the following year.

These meetings allowed Alan to develop, and to get into print, views on the dialogue which he had already struggled with for eighteen years. "Socialism," he wrote, in a collection of essays on the Dialogue, "is a movement of political action against a social order which discriminates against some human beings in order to maintain and extend the wealth and power of others…Those discriminated against…constitute millions of poor working people throughout the world…In Christian terms they are 'the least of my brethren', those to whom the prophets drew attention. I cannot as a Christian ignore this or pretend that it does not matter or leave it to others to attempt to do something about it. I must endeavour to bring this discriminatory order of society to an end and to replace it by one which is free from this evil." He argued that though Socialists had behaved badly at times this was no more a reason for leaving the Communist Party than religious persecution, witch-hunting and anti-Semitism were reasons for leaving the Christian Church. When people asked whether he found it difficult to be both Christian and Communist he replied that he found it difficult both to be Christian and to be Communist, and both together.

We have seen that the concern for nurture was the central point behind the Parish Meeting and it was here that Christianity and Communism came together. Like Péguy he did not want to see the political converted to the sole end of human being – his whole life, in fact, was a protest against this. If 'Mystique' was for Péguy the conjunction of the Spirit of God at work in the world with the activities of human beings in the founding and practice of their institutions, then 'Politique' was a rejection of that conjunction, a choosing to go it alone. It thus became an idolatry, ready to generate its own false mystique. Exactly so, Alan believed, Marxism had become trapped in dogma. Defection from such an arrested Marxism could only be a tribute to Marx, and within the Party he always remained an obstinate free thinker.

When Alan finally left Sheffield in 1969 Alderman Bingham, one of the old Labour stalwarts of Sheffield City Council, wrote to him, "We shall miss you from the city." What was it that Alan had actually contributed? Being a member of the Communist Party, like being a member of the Church of England, makes a person susceptible to the charge that it makes no difference to practical politics, to the ways in which people live, a charge Alan and Delia were only too aware of. As they trudged up the hill from Attercliffe one day after a branch meeting, he remarked to her that they now seemed to have two lost causes on their hands!

We have to ask, though, about the importance of radical minority groups in the whole social fabric. They help puncture complacent attitudes and keep up pressure on the groups nearest to them to be true to their founding inspiration. Similarly, in keeping the peace, the effect of the protests of small groups like that which marched through Sheffield in 1958, feeding later into CND, should not be underestimated. We simply do not know what would have happened if people had not concerned themselves with these matters and we cannot afford to presume that had nothing been done, results would have been just the same. Cynicism about the importance of small, minority, more or less anonymous, groups is particularly odd when it comes from Christians. For are not the whole of our Scriptures a celebration of precisely such groups? "God chose what the world counts foolish in order to put to shame what the world considers strong," says Paul.

Again, many of Alan's contemporaries could not understand why he stayed in the Party after Hungary, after Kruschev's revelations about the Purges, after Czechoslovakia. The answer is similar to reasons for staying within the Church of England. Membership of an organisation gives a framework for collective action, and structures the international dimension of a particular commitment. The question whether membership is more of a help or a hindrance to one's chosen praxis always remains. The Communist Party certainly obscured the initial vision of Marx, but then the Church obscured the initial vision of Jesus! Alan stayed loyal to both because he believed in the redeeming power of that initial vision, whether of the creation of a society where no one is exploited, and where the earth is given to share, or of a society where human beings are brought together and enabled to find reconciliation under the love of God. Loyalty to both was an expression of that conviction that 'salvation' can be found only in particular things, and not in general and abstract. And what else does it mean for the Word to become flesh?

1. BUBER, M. *Between Man and Man.* Fontana, 1968

9
A WAY OF
BEING IN THE WORLD

One day the Kotzker asked his Hasidim, "What does praying in earnest mean?" They did not understand him. He continued, "Is there anything that should not be done in earnest?"

THE RABBI OF KOTZK

A theologian is one who prays, and one who prays is a theologian

EPHRAIM THE SYRIAN

IN July 1969 Alan and Delia left Sheffield and moved to Gosforth, in Cumbria, an ancient village famous for the beautiful Norse cross in the churchyard, now standing in the shadow of the Sellafield Nuclear Plant. There, in a tiny cottage, with his library expanded into a long, low stone building adjoining, Alan began a third distinct phase of his life's work. He began to write, and four books appeared, the fruit of the experience of marriage, of his life in both parish and party, and of a lifetime of hard study. All the books were laboriously written and rewritten in longhand through many drafts. The first of these, *Yes to God*, which was published in 1975, established his name for a wide audience, won the Collins Religious Book Prize the following year, and has since been reissued as a 'modern classic'. This book, dedicated to Delia, drew on his thirty-five years of parish experience, and in particular the experience of marriage. In a way which was new to most people it explored the relation of praying to politics, sexuality and literature.

A book on the French poet and socialist Charles Péguy followed two years later, reflecting on the central issues of Alan's own life – *mystique* and *politique*. In 1980 came a book on

Christianity's relation to Judaism, *The Night Sky of the Lord*
which took up concerns which ran back to student days at Wells.
It was this book which produced the biggest public response,
generating a large correspondence with Jews, Christians and
non-believers. Seven years later appeared a very abbreviated
version of a book on John's gospel, *The Scaffolding of Spirit*, in
which that gospel was grasped as poetry. John was always Alan's
'canon within the Canon', the heart of his reading of Scripture –
especially as opposed to Paul, whom he could never abide.

Over three years he also compiled his great 'Book of Days'
where a reading and a picture for reflection were found for each
day of the year from the whole wealth of the European tradition.

For much of this time, and until within six months of his
death, Alan was travelling the length and breadth of Britain
preaching, speaking at conferences, giving courses for churches
and ordinands, and leading retreats. His diary lists more than
eighty churches, universities, and other centres at which he
spoke in these years, many on several occasions.

The end of his city ministry found him one of the best known
and most respected spiritual teachers of his time, constantly in
demand, always challenging, always fresh, able to reach the
unchurched like almost no other contemporary. This was partly
because his own spirituality was so profoundly rooted in secular
sources. In the list of eighty-seven 'helpers and teachers' which
he compiled towards the end of his life, only seven were
theologians. Four were Jews, six wrote on 'the spiritual life', the
rest were almost all poets, novelists and historians, and thinkers
on the margins of philosophy and theology such as John
MacMurray, Miguel de Unamono, or Julian Green. Pevsner,
and Henry Adams' work on Gothic Cathedrals, were a
permanent source of inspiration. What, then, was the shape of
the theology which emerged from this schooling?

Of Péguy, whom in his spirituality he so much resembles,
Alan wrote that he turned everything into a question of prayer,
and this is profoundly true of his own work. Alan's theology is an
arch between, on the one side, the living community, the Parish
Meeting, from whom he received his stimulus and for whom he
wrote, and on the other, the question of prayer. The arch
between these is above all a celebration of God in ordinary, or,

to use the technical term, of incarnation. For that very reason it is always a call to action. A number of themes and emphases characterize everything that Alan writes, from beginning to end: an insistence on honesty, and the need for truth; a hatred of fantasy; a struggle with the significance of sexuality for what is usually called 'our spiritual life'.

The key words of the whole are imagination, engagement, passion, and silence – words which seek to be 'the most honest we can find'. Prayer is what brings them together. It helps us to respond to everything that comes our way, Alan wrote, out of imaginative, sensitive, integrated, many-sided awareness of the time, event and question at hand. It is, in the words of Dumitriu, a way of being in the world – a way of being characterized by both engagement and passion. Reformulating Kant's famous duality of concept and intuition, Alan insists that engagement without passion is a heartless hoax, a mere formality, whilst passion without engagement is a display of fireworks, a waste of energy. The job of praying is to refuse to be disengaged. Our engagement seeks to respond to God's engagement and in this way the prayer of the Church forms part of the ongoing action of the incarnation.

Alan might have been expected to write more directly on politics, but this is to presuppose a separation of religion and politics which Alan himself refused. The one difference between the Church and the Party, he said, was that in the Church people prayed. To the extent that the Church was not a praying body it failed. He quoted von Hügel's review of Troeltsch's great work on the *Social Teaching of the Christian Churches*. It was, said von Hügel, "strangely thin, abstract, hypothetic, indeed subjectivist in many of its favourite terms and connotations," and this was because it missed entirely the rich content of spiritual life. It was because this had been, from the beginning, so central to his life, that Alan could never have been merely a politician, any more than he could have been merely a writer on spirituality.

"We have the same respect for Blake's philosophy," wrote T. S. Eliot, "that we have for an ingenious piece of home-made furniture: we admire the man who has put it together out of the odds and ends about the house. England has produced a fair number of these resourceful Robinson Crusoes." However it

may be for Blake, Eliot here acutely characterizes the nature of
Anglican theology. Like Anglo-Saxon philosophy, it is empiricist
in orientation, insisting on beginning and ending with experience, mistrustful of doctrines and speculation, at the end of
the day workmanlike and resourceful. Eliot went on to say that
"we are not really so remote from the Continent, or from our
own past, as to be deprived of the advantages of culture if we
wish them." Thomism, and the work of Calvin, Schleiermacher,
Hegel and Barth have all from time to time borne on English
theology but never in such a way as to produce an orthodoxy.
Alan is precisely such a resourceful Crusoe – hostile to speculation, insistent on beginning with praxis, his world view put
together from a vast range of Jewish and Christian thinkers, and
even, through Iris Murdoch, from Plato.

A far more important resource, for Anglicanism, has been the
English poetic tradition, not simply the 'religious' poets, like
Donne or Herbert, but the whole canon, and above all Shakespeare. "It is to the poets we must go," Alan said in a retreat
address towards the end of his life, "if we are to recover purity of
speech and breadth of imagination and delight in the Lord –
those three necessary elements of true prayer."

For most of his life Alan read Shakespeare from end to end in
the course of each year, and believed that English people needed
to learn to read him as they did the Psalms. He set out his
reasons for this in a paper he gave four years before his death.
Shakespeare lived in an age of bewildering change and his work,
Alan believed, must be understood as the counter-attack of the
Spirit.

In the Histories Shakespeare had sought to respond to where
his country was politically at the beginning of the seventeenth
century, and he saw the cloud of civil war already on the
horizon. Burchardt believed that history found its finest source in
poetry, and in Shakespeare history is a poetic activity. Not only
impending strife, but the rise of the individual, the nation state,
the priority of commodities, are all found in the Histories.

In the Comedies he turned to the relations of men and
women, the depths and ambiguities of erotic love. Romantic love
is the acting out of released imagination. It takes the most
meaningful element of human life, that of sexual love, to play

out the approaches to it in courtship. What he is concerned with is getting beyond appearances, and Alan believed that the essence of the Comedies was religious perception.

In the Tragedies we come to the silence beyond words. He reckoned with human evil and destructiveness at its very worst. Evil is not a problem to be solved; it is to be endured, out-lived, out-died.

In his final plays he turns to the 'new world', where, in each case, a young girl plays a decisive role. In these plays the length of time envisaged is increased: twelve to twenty years in *The Tempest* and *Cymbeline* and sixteen years in *The Winter's Tale*. This extension of time makes possible words like patience, endurance, long-suffering, grace, hope, fulfilment, resurrection. They are closely to do with living to maturity, to ripeness, to meaningfulness, which depends on grasping the significance of extended experience. It does not ignore the past, but utilises memory as an important factor in the spiritual life. Finally redemption is, as Prospero says, by prayer. Thus in the Shake-spearian corpus almost every aspect of the human condition is held up to us for reflection and rumination.

It is this intuitive reckoning with where God is to be found in human culture that saves Anglican theology from sterility and dullness. The training of clergy in the Anglican Church has, on the whole, shared in the anti-intellectualism of English culture and at worst this can produce a clergy scarcely theologically iterate, whose boast it is that they have no time to read. At best what emerges is a distinctive theology, earthed in the parishes and in local and national culture, and free from the dogmatism of confessional traditions. Alan stands absolutely squarely in this tradition. His theological roots are set deep within the Catholic Crusade, which means in the work of F. D. Maurice, Gore, Scott Holland, and all their antecedents, but they are nourished by a profound and continuous study of European history, art and literature. Though Alan's political roots were in Old Dissent he had much of William Morris's romanticism about the Middle Ages, and a sense of the need for beauty and sacred space was an important part of his spirituality. When Eamonn Duffy's revisionist account of the Reformation, *The Stripping of the Altars*, appeared in his last year he felt that it confirmed what he had

believed all his life. As much as he loved the men of the Putney
debates, so much he loathed the rationalism and reduction of
everything to 'the Word' of much Reformed worship. This side
of the Reformation he regarded as a catastrophe of the first
order.

The product of this synthesis is a strikingly fresh, clear, and
absolutely honest theology: the line from Padraic Pearse's great
poem *The Fool* crops up again and again, that we must not
'bargain nor huxter' with God. Everything in the tradition is
submitted to scrutiny, is read through the 'hermeneutic of
suspicion'.

Alan was aware, as rather few of his contemporaries were
especially the theologians, that the failure to take class seriously
is what makes both our theology and our spirituality 'poor and
mean', and he sought always to bear it in mind whilst writing. As
one who struggled in prayer for an entire lifetime he was
necessarily 'a theologian', but he never belonged to the guild
and his theology is marked by a a profound suspicion of dogma.
"It proved easier for Christians to think and speak lengthily of
the persons of the Godhead than to envisage human society in
terms of persons," he remarked tartly in *The Scaffolding of Spirit*
With Edwin Muir he suspected that words about God obstructed
the living Word taking flesh, and in that way were partly to
blame for the catastrophe of the Holocaust. He loved John's
gospel because he believed the author was wary of over-
theologizing the person of Jesus, and suspicious of the theological
acumen of Paul. Theology, he felt, very easily deflected the
Church from its real purpose, the preaching and embodying of
the Kingdom. In the face of the mystery of God "we are tempted
to burble," he said in his last address, "to gas on – no one more
so than theologians…but their misuse [of words] must not put us
off." It was one of the tasks of praying to stop this happening.

Alan was insistent that in praying we should not first begin by
trying to get straight the question "To whom do we pray?" Walt
Whitman addresses his poems to the unknown reader, "You
whoever you are." In the same way we pray to God – beginning
by jumping in and waiting for acquaintance to come later. On
the flyleaf of one of his personal prayer books was the remark of
a Victorian priest: "Prayer: I get down on my knees and hope

for the best." Praying, Alan believed, is not a problem to be solved but a venture to be lived.

He was led to write on prayer in the first place by a demand at a Parish Meeting that he should 'teach them to pray'. It took him aback, for he had assumed they were all praying merrily, but it also gave form, intellectually, to his life's work. The first result of this request was the Prism pamphlet, *On Praying*. Alan was impressed by a suggestion of Teilhard de Chardin's, that we are surrounded by a 'theosphere' in somewhat the same way as we are conditioned by the earth's atmosphere. Physically we live in a situation where atmospheric pressure governs our lives, and changes in the pressure affect our moods without our being aware of something having been 'done' to us. The presence of God can be conceived analogously and there are certain recurring 'moments' in human life when we unconsciously acknowledge this.

There is first of all the moment when we need to say "Thank you", or "Thank God", the spontaneous grateful recognition of something done and said which may come at a moment of release from anxiety or tension, or through the sudden disclosure of a good, wonderful and lovely thing. We have to give that moment's gratitude a chance to germinate and send down roots into our being so that thankfulness becomes the very texture of our life. For that to happen we have to look long at and sift our experience of life, like panning gold in gravel, by deliberately rehearsing it, deepening our gratitude and extending our recognition of its existence. The lists which Alan compiled, of his teachers, and of more than four hundred friends, were part of this attempt to say 'thank you'. It taught him, he wrote, "to see our personal lives not as pitiful threads soon to be snapped and forgotten – but as threads woven into an amazing tapestry of life. To pray is to try and extend that emotion, to come back to it and deepen it. This practice teaches us our indebtedness. The phrase: What have we which we have not yet received?" was frequently on his lips.

A second moment is in the cry – "O, how wonderful!" the cry of recognition from both Ferdinand and Miranda in *The Tempest*. This is the moment of sheer delight, when the beauty and goodness of some event, person or place makes us exclaim.

We have to extend and deepen our delight into real celebration. To cry for joy is as important for the right evaluation of our life as our food. To delight in the Lord is the very condition in which God gives us our heart's desire.

Another moment is recognized when we say "God help me" or "For Christ's sake". This is the moment of need, when we are frightened, anxious, distressed, or in pain. This is a cry in a situation or moment when the circumstances threaten to over whelm us, when we are on the edge of despair, if not despairing – when we have nothing but a cry left in us. Human beings are moved to cry, from infancy onwards. What does "Let our cry come unto Thee" mean if it does not tear at our flesh and spirit? We have to learn to become more aware of the pain of the world and feel it. We have to learn how to grieve. This recognition, most often wrung from us, is again something which we can extend by reflection, using every gift of the imagination. Our own felt need is the starting point but we can learn to pray this way for others.

Another moment is, "I'm sorry", or "Forgive me", behind which lies a sense of shame. This is the moment when we are overwhelmed by our folly and wickedness, when we face the bankruptcy of our desires and well meant intentions, when we are truly shocked by our iniquity and cry out to be cleansed and refashioned. It is precisely because we are not intended to live burdened by guilt that being sorry to the end of our lives is part of our agenda, both as a community and as individuals. Part of the concern of *The Night Sky* is to argue that we cannot authentically be Church unless we bear the Holocaust constantly in remembrance, and that we need something in the liturgical calendar, a 'Yom Ha'Shoah', which enables us to do that.

The next moment can be expressed in Othello's dying line "The pity of it", or as we say so often, "Oh, what a pity": the heartbreaking sense of something good and beautiful destroyed, spoiled, wrecked, the blighting of hope, the destruction of the good, the horror that evil has had its way – that has carried us beyond grief to pathos – the concern of the soul to find in God a transcendent suffering that vindicates the broken-heartedness of the creature. This, Alan suggests, is where we come nearest to God's attitude to what goes wrong. He says 'pity' as much as we do – "Like as a father pitieth his own children." This is the use of prayer to deepen our compassion, to put us alongside our fellow human beings. The sense of pity has to enter our prayers so that we become full of pity. We have to deepen the sense of shared pity to come near to the Passion of Christ.

Finally, there is "I'm through", "Over to you", "Into your hands I commend my spirit." This is the moment of exhaustion when we are flat out and beaten. The particular importance of this moment is that whenever we pray it we are, as it were, rehearsing for our death, when we commit ourselves to God. As Hamlet puts it, "If it be now, 'tis not to come; if it be not to come, it will be now; if it be not now, yet it will come. The readiness is all." It is part of the wholesomeness of praying that we recognize that this belongs to the fabric of life as God has given us to live it. As we have to give up one thing after another in advancing age we know that we are for ever in the mind of God.

Learning to extend these moments, which is learning to pray, is a lifetime's education. It begins first of all by learning to be *attentive*, the attitude inculcated by Alan's father in the meadows of Staffordshire. In, through, and beyond those impulses to cry out there is the most fundamental impulse of all – the hunger, thirst, desire, drive to love – the energy and passion of the soul in its seeking of God. It can be distorted and degraded and it can be both redeemed and redeeming. It is the supreme task of prayer to enable that love to find its true expression, to withstand the distortions, to eliminate the impurities. To learn the language of the heart – the language of loving – is the business of praying. "It is the language that our hearts want to learn – yearn to learn – the only true satisfying language we can learn – with its necessary silences and its expressions born out of experience – so that we may be one with Him and all His works – in true communication and communion."

The distinction which Coleridge sketched in *Biographia Literaria* between fantasy and imagination was fundamental to his understanding of prayer. Imagination, said Coleridge, "brings the whole soul into activity," whereas fantasy represents escape from reality, refusal of engagement. For this reason he could not allow that Tolkien was a good teacher for the young.

Christianity, he believed, easily became a romantic religion, pro-
ductive of illusions, enabling people to be sentimentally attached
to things which made few demands on them. Fantasy objects or
idols, he said, in his last address, "impede the fuller delight of
imagination…idolatry arrests and suffocates spiritual growth."
Fantasy is a way of unreality, cowardice and deceit, manifesting
itself in sentimentality and romanticism, distorting the imagery it
employs to achieve instant and plausible response. As such it is
part of 'anti-prayer'.

Prayer and anti-prayer, as Alan understood them, are what
shape the person we become. Just as we can extend and deepen
the sorrow, thanks, shame, wonder and so forth, in true prayer,
so we can extend and deepen bits of deceit, malignity, contempt,
cruelty, arrogance, hardness and lasciviousness. We are what we
pray, or we become what we pray. To give priority to anti-
prayer, which Alan identifies largely with fantasy, is to choose to
destroy our humanity. The antidote to such destructive fantasy is
firstly *attention*, learning to see, and secondly the cultivation of
the imagination, through which, according to Blake, we can per-
ceive and respond to the Glory of God.

Prayer, Alan insists over and over again, means paying
attention, seeking the truth, elucidating the truth of our lives, a
discipline which has to be learned, and which the artists and
poets are there to teach us. It is they who can open our eyes to
the truth of neglected things so that, as Ruskin understood,
looking at pictures and sculpture is not a luxury for aesthetes but
a demand to be more engaged with reality. The severance of
theology from the arts was a key part of the difficulty the Church
faced.

Similarly, what the poet seeks to do is to make available the
means of cleansed perception which enable people to see with
new intensity into the life of things, to enable words to become
bearers of the Word, to permit the Word to take our flesh and
dwell among us, to speak the words that hallow all that God
has given and human beings have received. The work of the
great poets is divine questioning. In them we have prophecy for
our day.

All works of art help us see with new joy and pain the truth of
the world which is ours, and making space for them fulfils in the

contemporary world something of the role of pilgrimage in the Middle Ages. Artists cannot do the work of prayer for us – prayer is not aesthetics – but the learning to see which is involved in serious consideration of art constitutes an essential preparation for it. Learning to be attentive is to prayer as primary school is to further studies.

The fundamental drive to pray, according to Alan, is neither joy nor pain but simply *hunger for reality*. "In both Art and Religion the war is on behalf of *reality* – a wholeness of vision which does not cramp and distort and sentimentalize or treat cynically what it perceives." The honesty which praying involves calls for continuous critical discernment. Facing up to the reality of urbanization, of our sexuality, or of the evil of the Holocaust, is accordingly our primary spiritual task. The camps are an illustration of what we know in any case from literature, that diabolism is a truth in life. In this diabolism Christianity has played a crucial part, insisting, for example, like one intemperate reviewer of *The Night Sky*, that it was 'the Jews' who crucified the Son of God. True prayer is about an honest facing up to this reality. "Between a fantasy that distorts and a literalism that simply reifies all objects and encloses us in such a world – both Art and Religion must endeavour to provide a breathing space for the Spirit and the Word."

The emphasis on reality, and the rejection of fantasy, led Alan to be extremely reticent in his views on the resurrection. He insisted that we cannot know what terms like new birth or new creation or immortality or eternity mean. Impressed both by the evidence of the immense size of the galaxies and by their seemingly accidental nature, he was inclined to take the almost Marxist line on resurrection, that each of us contributes what little we can to the historical process before returning to cosmic dust. Most conventional teaching on the resurrection he saw as yielding to the temptation to fantasy rather than imagination. In the same vein he wrote a reproving letter to a professor of New Testament whose speciality was apocalyptic, asking what earthly use it was. At the same time it has to be said that his writing 'breathes resurrection'. Notes on *Cymbeline* written in his last year perfectly express it. In the face of tragedy what Shakespeare offers is poetry in its 'alterity' – "a hint, a gesture, an arrow

loosed towards some 'all reconciling future'." Beyond this
hopefulness Alan was not prepared to go.

If true religion is about the reality of human life then true
prayer is the celebration of it. To pray in this way we need
silence, not the silence of mystical treatises, but the silence of
good conversation, which allows us to be alert rather than
apathetic, serene rather than fretful, open-minded rather than
fearful or defensive. If prayer is a form of conversation, then
conversation without silence is gossip, and this cannot be prayer.
We need silence all the more because we live, as Steiner put it,
"in a wind tunnel of gossip," where silence is vehemently fended
off. Preaching at Pentecost Alan took the text: "God is in
Heaven, thou upon Earth, Therefore let thy words be few." We
need to be delivered, he said, from spendthrift, idle, presump-
tuous use of words, pious affectations and dishonest commu-
nications, and rejoice in recognizing the miracle of speech. He
himself knew absolutely no gossip. He was so refreshing as a
conversation partner because he was always concerned with 'the
heart of the matter'. Only silence, he believed, allows us to pay
that attention to the condition of the other person, the assump-
tions of our own lives, our position in society, and the social class
we belong to, which is prayer. "The work of Christ consisted in
His obedience to, his unswerving trust in, the *Silence he called
Father*," he said in an address. "The world in which we live is a
world in which God is silent. But it is filled with the Word of
God – and it is for us who live by that Word to learn in silence to
listen to it."

Alan recognized, of course, that much talk of the need for
silence came from and addressed a cultivated élite who did not
have to labour for their daily bread. But the need for silence is
not precluded by the working and living conditions of most
people, even those on the margins of the shipyards of Barrow or
the steel works of Sheffield. Prayer begins with attention, and we
need to be silent in order to listen.

Another way of putting this is to say that prayer is the focusing
of all our attention so that it can lead to creative action. Prayer
and action are related like faith and works in the letter of James
– there cannot be one without the other. We can be instructed in
prayer by looking at the artist Francis Bacon's *Studies for a*

Crucifixion, but "what matters for praying is what we do next." Praying is not just contemplation, which stops short with looking at something, because we are not here to be spectators but to be involved with divine intention, which is why the petition, "Your will be done," forms part of the Lord's Prayer. When praying ceases to engage us with the society in which we live, when we become shockproof to the iniquities and cruelties it admits, and too timid or careless to seek for redress, then worldliness wins the day. Prayer sends us to think and work out what needs to be done. All that we pray must be securely tied to the question, "Where is your brother?" The horizons of the Church, he said, must be as wide as life itself, and receptive of all that enters human experience. "It must certainly enlarge our sense of guilt just as much as it should reinforce our need to hope and love. What it must not allow is a covering up or a silence about the terrible things like the Holocaust or genocide – or the contemptuous treatment of any persons whatsoever. A spirituality which loses sight of any of God's children is already condemned and stands in need of penitent renewal." It is through prayer that the Word becomes flesh. It does this by providing the process of digestion for experience – transforming experience so that it does in fact become nourishing – in a process of ruminating, connecting and resisting.

Prayer is concerned with making meaningful all that has passed through our experience, both the detail of our daily life, as also the wider canvas of human history, and setting everything in new perspectives. On the shelf in his study Alan kept a photograph of one of Michelangelo's unfinished sculptures. This to him suggested a way of looking at prayer and the terror of history. To pray was to seek the lines of God's emergent work in what appeared to be formless. Under the mind's tooling of the words and experiences of daily life some form may be given to things hidden there and in this process revelation occurs. Thus the book on the Holocaust provided, Alan said, "first of all material for praying." We cannot perhaps give an answer to the question of theodicy, of why suffering and evil are to be found at all levels of life, but it is in our power to pray in the face of unanswerable things.

Alan spoke of prayer as a 'kind of resisting', Jacob wrestling with the angel, wrestling with the absolutely intractable facts of history and refusing to let go until a blessing is wrung from them. Like an artist the one who prays endeavours to redraw the picture, correcting the distortions, perceiving new immensities, making sharper and clearer what is becoming obscured. In 1966 the Parish Meeting asked the question, "What difference does praying make?" The answer was, it creates an attitude towards all living – which is hopeful; it relates all living to God through Christ; it builds reserves with which to face living; it savours experience and gets the most out of it. It is in this way that prayer is political. Prayer is the refraction of the mundane, the day to day, in the prism of God. It puts the question to every political programme or structure as to whether it is good enough for the children of God, whether it truly establishes justice and mercy. The most insidious enemy of true religion, he believed, was the unreality that does not face the whole drama of human life – the dark and the light, the tragic aspects, the demonic, the wasteful, the religious pietism which lends a happy ending to the story when we do not know what it is to be. Shallow optimism, he insisted, is not Christian hope. What is required of us is generosity of spirit, width of sympathy and imagination, a magnanimity that carries us beyond the mean and narrow way of seeing things, whether they are social, political, theological or sexual.

Because it is concerned with all reality prayer is part of sexuality. "I could never make love with a man who said his prayers before going to bed," remarks one of Barbara Trappido's characters in *Brother to the More Famous Jack*. But prayer and sexuality belong together, Alan insisted, because the experience of 'falling in love' prompts us to notice, pay attention, yearn to communicate at ever deeper levels. He took from Suzanne Lilar the point that sexual love is not something needing to be sanctified but is sacred in itself. Sexuality, which includes not only the erotic but parenthood, marital breakdown, loss of a partner, and a great range of sexual problems, constitutes life itself for most people and any spirituality which ignores such things, or indeed denigrates them, is bound to be impoverished. People need to know how to pray them, or, since the relationship of prayer and play is now much better understood, how to play them out in an affirmative way. We underestimate the gravity of our predicament as human beings if we suppose that the relationship of the sexes does not form part of the material for prayer. Sexuality is part of the creative will of God at work in humankind and in it we are looking at the revelation of love. It is eros which teaches us how to glorify God in every cell of our bodies so that it can itself form an act of prayer.

In all of his books he turned to the creative role of women. "On or about December 1910 human character changed," wrote Virginia Woolf. In the work of women novelists from George Eliot onwards he saw the first major instalment of a long overdue correction of male perceptions of life. "Our spiritual insights no less than our human relationships have been disastrously starved of that which only women could give," he wrote. Women stand closer to both birth and death than men do, and to that which embraces them both, love. Our task therefore is to learn from the poets, novelists and singers who are working out their calling as women in today's world.

Prayer is again a kind of connecting. E. M. Forster's 'Only Connect!' is another phrase which constantly recurs in the notebooks, and he believed *Howard's End* to be one of the key prophetic texts of the century because of what it has to say about both individual and community. We pray in our inner chamber, but we pray also as a body. Praying is essentially an activity of communion and fellowship and is properly understood as part of the total response of creation to its maker. It is this because we are what we share. Péguy's attachment to the saints, Alan suggests, was nothing but an extension into the total history of humankind of his basic faith in God. The liturgy exists partly to foster this sense. 'Anamnesis', remembering, fits us in to the whole body, for those who have gone before us are not dead but 'alive in him'. Anamnesis is the representation of things done and said that they may be here and now operative in our midst: it is the heart of the poetic and sacramental understanding of life.

The practice of praying over the names of all those who had played a part in his life, and of all his teachers, was part of this. It underscored the sense that there is nothing we have not received, or, as Edwin Muir put it, "I am a debtor to all." It was part of the task of prayer, Alan believed, to cultivate the sense of life as a continuous thing. Our sense of personhood is included in this, for it is both a recognition of our total indebtedness on the one hand and our total requiredness on the other. He believed that praying over the names had taught him to recognize that individualism is a sheer impossibility, for we are woven into that "amazing tapestry of life." The very word 'individual' was a trip wire which could provoke Alan to fury, as many preachers found to their cost. "The word that expresses the truth of our nature is the *person*...we share in the humanity which Christ took upon Himself. We share in it because we are someone's child, someone's brother or sister, someone's parent perhaps, someone's friend, someone's neighbour, a cell in the Body of Christ...Looked at from this angle the individual is a sorry, meaningless, fragment and it is an affront to the glory of the Humanity that the Logos took upon itself to describe our being in individualistic terms."

The theology which this praying yields is above all that of the Spirit at work in the world. This is the natural focus of a parish priest struggling both to speak of God and to discern the reality of God in the day to day lives of his area and of his congregation. The most characteristic mark of this theology, and its most deeply impressive aspect, is its grasp of where God is in *ordinary* life, and the celebration of this ordinariness. The hidden God is no esoteric theme but a way of speaking of God here in this kitchen, in this marriage, in this friendship or enmity, in this movement of people struggling for better facilities in their own area. It was the rooting of and returning to all these concerns in prayer which ensured that they did not become trivial. In Péguy Alan found a tremendous affirmation of the local earth, the local countryside, which he himself cherished for many parts of Britain. In Britain, he believed, it was above all Blake who knew that 'everything is holy' in this way.

This celebration of ordinariness is summed up in the Incarnation. Alan's Christology shares the duality of much Christian Socialist teaching. On the one hand the Incarnation, God taking flesh, is an axial point, and it was entirely natural that the BBC should twice ask him to do Christmas broadcasts. The most neglected aspect of our praying, he wrote, concerns the implications of the doctrine of the Incarnation. "Only that which is incarnate may be properly called Christian."

The implications of the Incarnation, as he understood them, were two-fold. First, the sharp particularity of obligation towards the poor and rejected gains its universal face in Jesus Christ. To be for Christ is to be for the Kingdom, justice and fullness of life for all, which is something sought for with the intensity of a lover. Secondly, it is a recognition that personhood must stand at the heart of our understanding of reality. The Incarnation teaches us the transcendent character of human life, that human activities are caught up in a great drive of cosmic proportions, and that each phase of history matters intensely.

On the other hand he disliked doctrinal controversy about the Incarnation. Such controversy, he believed, centring attention on doctrine rather than practice, rendered Jesus safe. There is a splendid, (and totally unjust!), comment in *Gather the Fragments*: "Augustine? I detest him! His treatment of women was so appalling that it overshadows all his theologizing. He refuses to allow that you can no longer separate Word and Flesh. Once separated, once you refuse the reality of the Incarnation, you are left with a theology that is merely a heap of words." The scorn implied in the final phrase was never far away in any discussion of theology or theologians.

Theology, he always insisted, had to be translated into the working terms of our personal and Church life. The job of the Church, in his view, was not to preach doctrines about Jesus but to further the new way of living sustained by the Spirit that he bestowed on them. The Kingdom Jesus preached signified a life to be laid hold of here and now within the kingdoms of the world, a leaven at work to change the hearts and minds of human beings.

Although the 'Yes to God' which is prayer was lived out in the first instance in the life of Jesus this does not mean we can equate the preaching of the Kingdom with the preaching of an exalted Redeemer. Christological doctrines limited what Jesus had done and was. To have elevated the Son of Man to princely thrones and altars at the expense of his homelessness is to have lost sight of something of profound importance in our understanding of our own condition. Jesus mined deeper into Israel's knowledge

of God, profound as that was, and in his own living showed wha
it was like to us. We cannot capture this lived reality in dogmas
and the attempt to do so forgets that the Jesus we seek is alway
striding on ahead of us.

"The business of treating other human beings as the sons and
daughters of God is the only real force of the Gospel," he said in
a retreat address in 1990. The Gospels themselves are insuffi
cient, signposts and not destinations. They point to thing
unsaid, things which they encourage us to expect, which lie
beyond, yet which bear upon our inmost life and the world in
which we live. Their insufficiency is entirely right because it i
this which demands we use the greatest of God's gifts – imagina
tion – if they are to function as they are supposed to and bring u
any distance along the road of which Christ is both the way and
the goal.

The focal point of Alan's devotion, he always candidly ad
mitted, was the 'Jesus our Leader' of the Catholic Crusad
prayer. The tension between this figure, who called people into
the Kingdom, and the incarnate Lord, from whom we learn
about God's immanence in all things, is never resolved. It wa
always on Jesus as Son of Man, the representative human being
rather than as Son of God, that he wanted to insist. Whils
having place for the uniqueness of Christ, in a non-trivial sense
nevertheless he could see God incarnate in all realizations of true
human being, just as every birth was, in Pasternak's words, 'an
immaculate conception'.

At the same time we have, entirely characteristically, this
entry from his last Diary. He refers to a thesis he had read which
imagined that all that was left of Shakespeare after a cultural
holocaust was the line from *King Lear:* "Never, never, never
never, never." "It has left me pondering from time to time on
what line from the Scriptures I would want to be left with if all
the rest perished. My choice, brooded over for a good many
years is, 'This is life eternal – that they should know Thee, the
only true God, and Jesus Christ whom thou hast sent'." Alan
was not a conventionally pious person. He never spoke of 'Jesus'
only of 'Jesus Christ' or 'Jesus of Nazareth'. All the same, the
centrality of this figure to his whole imaginative and spiritual life
could never be in doubt to those who knew him.

For the cover of *Yes to God* Alan chose a photograph of a 'crucifix' made from an eighteenth century man trap, used in the chapel of King's College, London, a photo he kept on his mantelshelf in much the same way as Barth kept the Grünewald *Crucifixion* above his desk. It summed up his whole approach to the death of Christ, which weighed on him as a mystery "not to be explained or resolved". As Holy Week advanced in Darnall, year by year, Alan retreated further and further into himself, became more and more surrounded by silence. This was because reflection on the Cross, for him, led to the heart of darkness. "Those who believe in God," wrote Unamono, "but without passion in the heart, without anguish of mind, without uncertainty, without doubt, and even at times without despair, believe only in the idea of God, and not in God himself." That despair was never far away. What was *redemptive* about it was the realization that the Passion was not a hurdle on the road to God, but the very road itself.

In the Three Hours Service he conducted at St Paul's Cathedral in 1983 he quoted Edwin Muir:

> Some day
> I know that I shall find a man who has done good
> His long life long, and is
> Image of man from whom all have diverged.

And he commented: "That is the nature of this journeying life to which we are called: to find *that* man's image, and in finding it, to lay hold of the meaning that properly belongs to life itself. What the Passion does is to set before us that true image of man – carrying those who witness it to the very limits of human response. It gathers up into itself *all* those things which in our own imperfect existence we nevertheless acknowledge to be of worth: the respect that is paid to another human being because he or she is human, the delight in beauty, the tenderness of affection, the joy of relationships honoured, the gentleness, compassion and mercy that prompts assistance, the kindness that flows out to sustain."

All the hallmarks of Alan's theology are here: the widest possible berth given to conventional atonement theologies, rooting in the realities of everyday, bringing us back to 'the way'. By doing the deed we know the doctrine.

The marks of the spirituality we need now, he concluded, at the end of the Péguy book, are amplitude, imagination, fidelity freedom and costliness. Alan always cheerfully confessed himself an amateur in the field of theology, and what his books leave us with are sketches, not great finished works of art. But in the attempt to address every area of human life, to discern God at work there, to measure everything by the revelation of the 'Yes to God' of Jesus of Nazareth, these are sketches which remain immensely challenging, and renewing of the resources by which we grow in humanness. We cannot, finally, ask more of any theology.

10
GATHERING THE FRAGMENTS

In me thou see'st the glowing of such fire,
That on the ashes of his youth doth lie,
As the deathbed whereon it must expire,
Consum'd with that which it was nourish'd by.

SHAKESPEARE

And when they were filled, he said to his disciples,
gather up the fragments that remain, so that
nothing is lost.

John 6.12

ALAN was ambivalent about the move to Cumbria, to say the least, but the letters of the first year are euphoric. "It's been marvellous to be in such country," he wrote to a friend in his first spring there. "The powdering of snow on the fells and on Scafell has been one great glittering mass…Curlews and plovers are fascinating to watch, and a pair of buzzards are always circling slowly over a coppice close at hand. The wild daffodils are beginning to come out now: before, snowdrops were thick in hedges like drifts of snow."

In the first years Alan still walked a good deal, following the path which ran up beyond the house to High Stile, or Pillar, and returning at a gentle pace. His enthusiasm for the place was matched by that for the local community: "Social life fairly *buzzes* in this valley," he wrote. "We find people most friendly." However, Alan was, from the moment of 'retirement', frequently away, leaving Delia alone for long stretches, a fact he later deeply regretted. Further, his sense of being driven remained with him: the need to write had become urgent. Just a fortnight after the euphoric letter just mentioned Delia is writing despairingly to the same friend telling her there is no point in coming to Wasdale at all, as Alan cannot possibly see her: "He's in a very strained patch, and has been since coming here." The sense of strain arose from the old need to have everything ready well in advance, which applied to all the retreat addresses he gave, and which left what he felt was insufficient time for the emerging book on prayer. The only time when he was truly relaxed was on holiday in the Pyrenees, where Alan read John Berger and Herbert Read, and enjoyed walking, and bathing in the ice-cold rivers. These, too, were the best times with Delia.

At the end of April 1974, after four energetic years during which *Yes to God* was written, Delia had a stroke. For some time Alan tried to care for her himself, but she had finally to be admitted to a home in Whitehaven, where she remained, barring brief trips home, until her death eight years later. In all that time Alan visited her each day, travelling by bus, except for one day when the snow was too heavy. For the whole period both of them continued the exploration of love, pain and forgiveness which their marriage had been. Alan began a diary in January 1978 which he kept until the day of Delia's death. On the fly leaf he wrote a short prayer, which began with words from the story of the feeding of the five thousand, "Gather up the fragments – that nothing be lost." "You said this, Lord, when the amazing abundance of your gifts was manifest, when men had all they needed…You have given, Lord, just such things to us in the Love that made us man and wife."

"I once thought in my careless way that we might grow old together, sitting quietly and peacefully by the fireside in our home. It was not to be. You prepared something else; for her something infinitely harder to bear, yet, I must believe, something more meaningful, more expressive of yourself, than anything else could have been – that she should be your servant in that hospital ward, and through distress and pain shine out with your goodness and love, herself gathering up and using once more the fragments gathered up. May I, so prodigal and so foolish, learn to do so too."

The diary records Alan's gratitude and delight for every sign of love and tenderness on Delia's part, for every joke shared.

Maintaining attention was difficult for her, but, "I am glad to God that she is there at all, and I speak to her even if it is but a fragment of the marvellous person that was her true self. This business of gathering up the fragments takes on a new pathos each day – but I would miss none of it." Each day Alan read Delia some poetry, or parts of favourite novels. Pain reduced her attention span, and yet she was able to respond, to echo the scraps of poetry Alan read her, to within a few weeks of her death. "You didn't come into the world to be a success. You came into the world to have a great heart and to suffer," Péguy wrote to a friend, in words which Alan applied to Delia. Whenever possible they went out to a nearby park and had tea, or a glass of wine, and played Mozart or Bach on the tape recorder. They also often shared the Eucharist there and Alan prepared a number of communion services for their time to-gether, 'the communion of married life', with opening sentences taken from a huge range of poetry and theological literature. The opening prayer ran:

"Father whose Glory fills all heaven and earth, and dwells be-tween a husband and wife, may we whom you have drawn and held together in your love, have hearts that are attentive to you here, and learn to live together with great joy, continuing in success and failure, in the darkness and the light, to put our trust in you."

The preface to the Confession notes that there is never a point of no return: "We have neglected to love each other, and to love others, with all our heart and mind and strength…Enable us to begin again." The dismissal was "You are living. You are loved. You are free."

In the prayer book of pictures and poems and extracts from novels which Alan put together for Delia was this fragment from Delia herself:

> Communion Sunday afternoons
> by bed. Ward B –
> How can I shew my
> thanks for all this
> that has happened
> and worked together

> for good –
> as we try to say
> Yes to God.

e. e. Cummings' affirmation was heavily underlined:

> i thank you, God, for this most amazing
> day: for the leaping greenly of trees
> and a blue dream of sky: and for everything
> which is natural, which is infinite, which is yes.

Frequently the only thing which Delia would say was, "I love you," over and over again.

In 1975, paralyzed on the left side, and in great pain from thrombosis, she wrote 'A Letter to a Friend' in which she tried to come to terms with "the jig-saw muddle of stroke and bed-wetting."

"I go over and over parts of Psalm 73 and now I know the writer must also have had a thrombosis and a stroke. In one of the modern translations it goes like this, 'When my heart had been growing bitter with pains shooting through my loins, I simply failed to understand my attitude to you was brutish. Even so I stayed in your presence. You held my right hand.' No use whatever, I have to be held on my left side…Be with Him – Mother Julian of Norwich again. But it means nothing unless when we say it we mean something about bedpans and entire crippled dependence on a nurse taking us to the toilet. Bladder and bowels must take their essential place in, 'Oh all ye works of the Lord bless ye the Lord.'

"You are loved: where does that come from? You are loved. In that lies the truth of your life. That love comes through a multitude of streams and becks now hidden now seen, 'til the great ocean is reached. My brook becomes a river, and my river becomes a sea."

The struggle to say 'Yes', a struggle against pain, a constant refinding of forgiveness and affirmation, continued to the beginning of 1982. Their last visit to the park together was on 31st January of that year. Shortly after that Delia developed flu, and it became clear she would not survive much longer. "Dear Lord, you have given me so much borrowed time to be with this beloved," Alan wrote on 13th February. She died on the 26th, "ceasing to breathe without effort, and looking so heavenly beautiful. Thanks be to God in *His* great mercy." She was buried in Gosforth Churchyard six days later, a day of sunshine, with snow on the hills. A flowering tree was planted in her memory, in the shadow of the ancient Norse cross. Two days before her death Alan went through the whole of their marriage service with her at her bedside, Delia joining in where she could. Alan put Kathleen Raine's poem *Parting*, which he described as the greatest love poem of the century, in this page of his Book of Days:

> Darling, this is goodbye. The words are ordinary
> But love is rare. So let it go tenderly
> As the sound of violins into silence.
>
> Parting is sad for us, because something is over,
> But for the thing we have ended, it is a beginning –
> Let love go like a young bird flying from the nest,
>
> Like a new star, airborne into the evening,
> Watched out of sight, or let fall gently as a tear,
> Let our love go out of the world, like the prayer for
> a soul's rest.

"Love outlasts and outreaches the death of the beloved," he had already written in *The Night Sky of the Lord*, "and opens to those who love a deathless relation." "Now she sleeps in this country churchyard in sight of the high fells she so loved," he wrote to a friend two weeks after the funeral: "What better?"

A profound reflection on the relations of men and women had been part of Alan's journey for more than forty years. This now more and more took the form of reflection on the relation with Delia. "What has my life amounted to?" he asks in his diary, at the beginning of 1992.

"The things given to me have been very rich: the use I have made of them not very good...It is to Delia that the good things have been mainly due. God has been infinitely patient and merciful with me: sparing me the disastrous consequences that might well have attended my foolishness and recklessness time and again through the years. The forty years of marriage were sustained by the Spirit to which Delia responded so largely and I myself intermittently. During her illness I learned something of this and I am deeply grateful for those later years."

The quality of living an examined life, with Alan from the beginning, became more rigorous as the years went by. "It has been a wonderful life that has been given to me," he noted at the beginning of 1991, "spoiled only by my selfishness, foolishness, self-indulgence."

"I regret these things all the more because they limited and warped my relations with people, twisted my responses to good things in life, made me less generous, less loving, less appreciative than I might have been. God has gone on being generous to me, and all too often I have been blind to this."

"How does a person like myself try to bring the tattered remnants of life into some sort of order?" he asks. "I am very conscious of its flawed character, increasingly so with the passage of time, and at this late hour there is not a great deal I can do about it." Alan's awareness of his 'Gemini like confusion' referred to this strong sense of failure rather than to any kind of double life. "A largely wasted day. God help me to recover my senses and begin again," runs one entry – this in a year when he gave more than twenty papers and addresses, read the whole of Shakespeare, and eighty novels! It referred also to the immense effort his self-discipline cost him. His passion for life could easily have taken other, more hedonist turns. His positive hatred of fantasy was doubtless because the lure of his own possible fantasy life was strong. It was a shadow side to which he said 'No', but which was costly to deny. As a young man he had dallied with the idea of becoming a monk. "Would it have given more consistency, more depth, more maturity, to my living?...I am conscious of my life's immaturities, its huge inconsistencies, its makeshift character." The question, though real, was certainly answered in the negative.

Throughout the eight years of Delia's illness Alan managed to go on writing, and the first three books appeared, though he accepted no engagements around the country. Although he was tempted, after Delia's death, to give up his lectures and addresses, he in fact quickly took them up again, and once more began writing – a huge, Péguy like, meditation on St John, published in drastically abbreviated form in 1987. After this, though he produced more papers, and set to work on a number of projects, no further book found its way to the publishers.

The death from cancer of his second son, Giles, in September 1990, was another bitter blow. After a distinguished career first in the civil service, and then at Church House as secretary to the Board of Social Responsibility, Giles had become Vicar of Over, near Cambridge where, like his father, he started the Parish Meeting. Father and son were temperamentally very different but Alan felt the warmest admiration for all that Giles had done. During Giles' last weeks Alan stayed with the family, and father and son found perhaps a deeper level of understanding than they had ever done before.

"Seeing Giles' face as he lay dead," he wrote in his diary, "I was overwhelmed. Never before have I seen a face so awesomely beautiful. It had an austerity and dignity such as one would hope that a man's life could come by – and this I felt to have been no accidental setting of his features but the attainment of his life – a gentle kindly achievement but of such rare dignity and sweetness that I could have wept for something approaching a thanksgiving to God." In his *Book of Days*, for the day of Giles' death, he included the final line of Hardy's *The Woodlanders*: "For you was a good man, and did good things."

Once again, Alan made a decision to decline further invitations to talk, which had become numerous again after Delia's death, but by the beginning of the following year he was back in action. Twice he was invited to do the Christmas meditation on BBC television, and one of the four programmes on the *Faith of Marxism*, presented by Marx's biographer, David McLellan, was devoted to his work in Sheffield.

The walks of the young man who once strode over the fells were slowly curtailed, though he insisted on walking the mile or so into Gosforth village until the very last, and loved to get into the shallow valley adjoining the house, the Bleng, to gather firewood and admire the flowers. His intellectual and critical faculties in no way suffered. Like Moses, his eye was not dimmed, nor his natural force abated, until almost the end. A succession of Gosforth clergy found him an intimidating, if invigorating, critic. Whilst Delia was still alive she could be heard remarking in a loud voice, after the passage from the *Epistle to Timothy* on the subordination of women had been read, "What Rubbish!" After a pleasant Eucharist in one of its modern forms, Alan would turn to the Vicar at the door and say, "Do you realize that the only person you prayed for by name is the richest woman in the world?" When the diocesan bishop preached on the story of the rich man his comment was, "You illuminated neither wealth nor, poverty!" "Felt lacerated," was his diary entry after one service.

With student groups the old fire was never lost. Speaking to undergraduates about the seventeenth century revolution, three years before his death, his interpretation of the Putney Debates was rubbished by the up and coming revisionist historians who wished to turn their back on the 'Marxist conception of history'. In the ensuing argument Alan was able to cite those seventeenth century debates, to which he had first been introduced by his mother, verbatim and at length. This period and its passions remained absolutely present to him as a key factor in understanding contemporary social reality.

He never ceased to learn or to be thrilled by new books and films. Peter Greenaway's film *Prospero's Books*, for example, left him full of questions and excitement. "You need more than one life!" was a recurring theme. He loathed the meanness of spirit of the Thatcher revolution, the repealing of the hard won gains of a century and a half of union struggle. "The evil that men do lives on after them," he noted in November 1990, under the heading 'Political prognostications'. "It will take a whole *generation* for the British society to get the poison of Thatcherism out of its veins." In the Gosforth area he was always part of the opposition to dumping nuclear waste in Sellafield. At village meetings on the question he would appear with awkward and well-informed questions for the nuclear industry spokesman, and people would turn and ask, "Who let *him* in?"

Though he was warmly and marvellously supported in the village he began to regret moving to so remote a place, especially as public transport cuts made Gosforth ever more difficult to reach. He missed the stimulus of art galleries, the theatre, and intellectual life, profoundly. Gosforth, unlike the coastal areas to the south and north, had been part of a Viking settlement, and Alan now felt the area retained much of its Norse character despite all the 'incomers', and with this he was not in sympathy. Frequent bad weather also depressed his spirits.

On a beautiful day in late September 1991 a large crowd of family and friends gathered at Carlisle Cathedral to celebrate the sixtieth anniversary of his ordination. His old friend Alan Webster spoke about the apostolic succession as the asking of God's questions, of those who speak truth from their heart and live criticized lives in order to stand for God's justice. Messages of congratulation were read from the Archbishop and from the Bishops of Sheffield and Manchester but in his reply Alan quickly pointed away from himself and spoke of the service of Him whom he sought to keep in view all his life.

In the addresses he gave on 'Waiting on God' before Easter in 1992 Alan noted the words of Dr Johnson: "Death, my dear, is very dreadful: let us think nothing more our care but how to prepare for it; that we know amiss in ourselves let us make haste to amend and put our trust in the mercy of God and the intercession of our Saviour." That sense of death, he noted, had largely disappeared – but not for him. In the last two years reflections on death become more prominent in his diaries. "I have throughout my life been greatly concerned, and probably over-anxious, to keep my appointments punctually and to be as well prepared as possible for the interviews, examinations and jobs to be done," he wrote in 1991. "For the last appointment I should like to be – not over-anxious – but as well prepared as possible too, and to do this with gratitude and thankfulness for all that I have been given to enjoy throughout my life: thankful to God who gave me this life, thankful for my parents who lavished such love upon me, thankful for beloved Delia and all that was given through our married life, thankful to my sons and their wives for their love and unfailing kindness, thankful for my grandchildren who have been such a source of delight, thankful for my teachers and friends in every place."

After Easter 1992 Alan suffered a small heart attack, but discharged himself from hospital after only two days, and was not a good patient! In September came a stroke which to some extent incapacitated his speech, and made writing difficult. The return to hospital was a completely different experience, and he had nothing but praise for the work of those who cared for him. The speech therapy which followed was something he enjoyed greatly, a return to childhood experience which amused him no end. The speech therapist had, she said, "never come across so many long words!" In the last phase, he wrote, we seem to be reversing the process of how we learned to speak and express words. "Many patients feel utterly hopeless, useless and *unable to find any meaning in their existence* at this stage. Then someone comes who breaks the monotony, the loneliness, the purposeless agonized waiting." The sense of "the need of a dying person to leave something behind – to give a little gift," became ever more present to him. "*One foot in Eden,*" he had written in his diary three years earlier: "I want to grow into that compassionate life – that sees the beauty, patience, heroism, love – however fragmentary – however swallowed up in the bitterness and tragedy and pain of existence – I want to live all my remaining days in that spirit, to seek it patiently and to learn how to value its beauty and goodness in all its brief fragmentary manifestations."

With the help of neighbours and friends Alan managed to hold his own, but with winter coming on he finally decided to go south and spend a third of it with each of his two sons, and with his daughter in law, Imogen. Travelling down by train, from Gosforth, at the end of November, he characteristically took himself off to the National Gallery the very day after arrival, to see a painting by Crevelli which contains one of our earliest pictures of a child playing, and which had always excited and moved him. The strain proved too much, and he suffered another heart attack in the evening.

There now followed three difficult weeks in hospital. Lack of oxygen to the brain made him awkward and even violent with family and nurses. And yet even then there were periods of great lucidity. Though his speech was difficult he was able, only eight days before his death, to range over Iris Murdoch's new book, the work of the American Marxist, Frederic Jameson, a production of Ben Jonson's *The Alchemist,* government policy on mines, as well as asking about all sorts of more or less distant acquaintance. It was a particular pleasure to him to receive communion from the woman Chaplain as he was an ardent supporter of the ordination of women. Hospital conditions made him disinclined to eat, which increased the chance of mental confusion, and in the face of patient pleading he resisted stubbornly. But then, with all his old humour, he turned and asked, "Which of the angels, do you think, is in charge of food?...I wonder what they think of all this!"

The day before his death he was discussing the constitutional question raised by the possible divorce of the Prince of Wales, and seemed to be stronger. He died peacefully on Monday 14th December, and was buried in Delia's grave on a morning of cold bright sunshine, five days later. Snow already decked his favourite Lakeland hills. He left instructions for his funeral in the cottage in Gosforth, which included a reading from John 14, a hymn of William Morris, and the version of the Jewish Yigdal, *The God of Abraham Praise*. Lines of Martin Buber's, from *Between Man and Man*, were used for the sentences: "This fragile life between birth and death can nevertheless be a fulfilment – if it is a dialogue. In our life and experience we are addressed; by thought and speech and action; by producing and by influencing we are able to answer. For the most part we do not listen to the address, or we break into it with chatter. But if the word comes to us and the answer proceeds from us, then human life exists, though brokenly, in the world." (1)

Two poems always on Alan's lips were included: Padraic Pearce's *The Fool*, and Edwin Muir's *One Foot in Eden:*

> What had Eden ever to say
> Of hope and faith and pity and love
> Until was buried all its day
> And memory found its treasure trove?
> Strange blessings never in Paradise
> Fall from these beclouded skies.

At the committal, words of Unamono's were used which had also been used at Delia's funeral: "God deny you peace and give you glory."

"Alan was a saint" – so the funeral address began, and those

who knew Alan best, who knew what could be his fierce
dogmatism, his stern judgment on political options he believed
dehumanizing, drew breath. Yet what this shows is rather the
need to redefine our understanding of sanctity.

Alan was a 'saint', one of the great cloud of witnesses we
celebrate on All Saints' Day, because like the forerunners
mentioned in the *Epistle to the Hebrews*, he never gave up hope,
in eighty-eight years never became cynical, or blasé, or thought
he knew it all. At the end of it he was still learning. In the last
two years he took up new books on sociology, anthropology and
theology with the thrill of entering a world unknown. He was a
saint in this sense because the passion for justice was never
dimmed, not to the last moment. He was a saint because he went
on loving, believing in the possibility of loving, despite all the
mistakes. "It is not because of men's successes in the roles that
the world acknowledges," he said at the fiftieth anniversary of
Hugh Bishop's ordination, "but in their many failures through
which they continue steadfastly in their faith, that they contribute most generously to the nurturing process."

Words Alan used of Péguy may once more be applied to him:
"Péguy is an impenitent foot slogger. He speaks most characteristically when he talks of beginning again." Having the courage
to begin again was, Alan insisted, one of the key aspects of any
understanding of prayer, but just because it characterized prayer
it applied to everything. In marriage, in relationships, in the
parish, in the party, in reading and in writing, one must always
be beginning again. Delia's steadfastness in beginning again after
every fall was one of the things those who came to her funeral
thanked God for, and this was something the two of them
shared. "When you get to my age," he wrote in his eighty-fifth
year, "you begin to realize that very many of the things you do,
you are doing for the last time. A fuller reflection may help you
to see that you are doing them for the first time – with that kind
of attention to them and awareness of their significance they
deserve. Life could be a texture of first times – new life made
evident."

"No easy companion, but a man inexhaustibly rich." The
words Alan used to describe Péguy sum up the feelings of many
of those who knew him, the great crowd of Communists and

Christians of all denominations, educated and uneducated, who turned up for his memorial service in Sheffield Cathedral at the end of January 1993. This richness sprang from his own *approfondissement*, going deeper in prayer. The old banner from Darnall Church, written in Chinese characters by Bishop Ting, hung over the pulpit: "Truth will triumph." In his last years, in an increasingly darkening political landscape, Alan frequently spoke of the need to be in the wilderness, "perhaps for thirty years" – but he never surrendered the belief that, as Milton put it in the Areopagitica, "If truth be in the battlefield, let none fear the issue of the conflict."

A message from Bishop Ting in faraway Nanking was read out at the service. For senior Anglicans Alan's joining the Party remained a mistake – "neither eccentric, nor prophetic, but a serious misjudgment," as one put it. The Chinese Bishop saw things differently. "Alan's joining the Communist Party was to me one of his ways to witness to Christ where he was not honoured, and against narrow-mindedness in the years of the Cold War. Like some Old Testament prophets, he was putting across a message from God by taking some symbolic actions."

The sense of failure which recurs so frequently in the diaries of his last years never mastered him to the extent of making him bitter or despairing. On the contrary, the courage to begin again remained the last word. He was, to the end, passionate, clear sighted, rigorously honest and engaged, living by the faith of Padraic Pearse's poem:

> Was it folly or grace? Not men shall judge
> me, but God.

1. Buber, M. *Between Man and Man,* Fontana, 1968, p. 119

TIM GORRINGE was ordained in 1972, and after serving curacies in Allerton and Oxford, worked in India from 1979–86. Since 1986 he has been Chaplain of St John's College, Oxford. He has had two books published by the SCM Press, *Discerning Spirit: A Theology of Revelation* (1990), which explores the question of how and where God can be found in today's world, and *God's Theatre: A Theology of Providence* (1991), which takes the image of God as theatre director (as exemplified by Peter Brook in *The Empty Space*), by which God is given a supremely active role and does not destroy or manipulate human autonomy.

ISBN 1 870652 21 5   £10·95

ISBN 1-870652-21-5

01095

9 781870 652216